TERRY RUMMINS

So, We Progress, Parkinson's and I

D1421858

Matador
9 Priory Business Park,
Wistow Road, Kibworth Beauchamp,
Leicestershire. LE8 0RX
Tel: 0116 279 2299
Email: books@troubador.co.uk
Web: www.troubador.co.uk/matador
Twitter: @matadorbooks

ISBN 978 1785892 899

British Library Cataloguing in Publication Data.
A catalogue record for this book is available from the British Library.

Printed and bound in the UK by TJ International, Padstow, Cornwall

Matador is an imprint of Troubador Publishing Ltd

For Doctor Howlett
a singular man
and a singular GP

CONTENTS

1
PROGRESSION

A life changing event can be sudden and dramatic. That is how my diagnosis of Parkinson's Disease, seemed to me. But a life changing event can also be gentle, insinuating itself tactfully into one's daily round. That is how I felt about the positive responses I received after publishing my first book.

When I started writing about my life with Parkinson's, I assumed that my experience would be very different from that of most other people who had the condition. My general reading about Parkinson's Disease had led me to this point of view. So, I was extremely surprised to learn from conversations with Parkinson's people who had read my book, that we have far more in common than I had originally thought. I was very heartened when I realized this and so I shall continue trying to describe my life with Parkinson's, as it progresses, in the expectation that what I say may be relevant to a fair number of people out there.

It is now thirteen years since I was diagnosed with Parkinson's Disease. As a reminder, this illness occurs when a very necessary chemical substance in the brain, a neurotransmitter called dopamine, is no longer available in the quantity that is needed. Cells that produce dopamine die off, are not replaced and in the natural course of events the Parkinson's person's condition will steadily deteriorate. Basically, the patient can gradually lose the ability to move and there can also be other, non-motor symptoms.

However, thanks to the discovery of powerful drugs, which act on the brain, there is help available, although so far no one has been able to prevent the progress of the illness. The first laboratory produced drug used to help people with Parkinson's, was levodopa and this continues to be the main source of relief for most people with Parkinson's. Levodopa was first used widely in the nineteen sixties and now, over fifty years later, it is still widely used. Other drugs have been produced over the years and they can be very helpful, although in my case nothing works as well as levodopa.

I cannot sufficiently express my gratitude for the existence of levodopa. When the drug works at its optimum, I can almost remember what it felt like not to have Parkinson's. However, an unusual characteristic of levodopa is that the patient's symptoms can change rapidly from 'On' (drug working well) to 'Off' (drug not working well or drug has worn off) with little warning. In my case, I generally have five or six of these fluctuations per day. Also, some unfortunate side effects of levodopa are that after approximately six years of taking this drug one can develop hallucinations and / or dyskinesias. So far I have not had any hallucinations and my dyskinesias are not particularly disturbing. But I'm ready!

There is no doubt that my movement, shaking, balance, fatigue, and verbal language have deteriorated during the past eighteen months. But it is equally true that this has been a rewarding, happy period for me as a whole person.

Jack, my husband, and I have continued to live for part of the year in France and part in the UK and in both countries we have continued our relationships with old friends and made new friends. It has been a productive time and I can't separate the progression of my Parkinson's from my progression as a whole human being. I have been aware of Parkinson's encroaching on more of myself. Yet, I have also been aware of myself encroaching on Parkinson's unquestioning assumption that it will make me a lesser person.

Five or six times over the past year I have been brought to the limit of my physical strength and energy in situations which could hardly have been called taxing. At these times, I have come to the point of being almost unable to move, because of general exhaustion, involuntary shaking and painful tightening of my muscles. For example, I needed to sit down urgently in the street in France a while ago because I was too exhausted to keep standing. Luckily, I found a low wall to sit on, but without this I would have had to sit on the pavement. These occasions have happened when I have been 'Off' or, as I call it, 'down'. My 'Offs' or 'downs' are now more intense than they used to be. Over the last eighteen months, I know that my Parkinson's has progressed.

I now define 'up' as being 'almost normal'. I say, 'almost' because I have a particular symptom that occurs most of the time when I am standing or walking . It is a feeling of physical instability, rather like being on a gently rolling ship. My sense of direction has worsened. I now bump, even more readily, into doorways, people and other large, conspicuous objects that most people would easily circumnavigate. The way I deal with these problems of instability and lack of a sense of direction is to take someone's arm at all times when I am walking outside. That way I minimize the possibility of accidents.

When I go 'down' I stoop and shake, my muscles tighten up and I move extremely slowly. Recently, the last of these, the slowness of movement (also called bradykinesia) has increased. When my bradykinesia takes over, every single physical task that I undertake seems almost impossible because of an overall feeling of heaviness and exhaustion. I can achieve some actions by breaking them down into smaller tasks, but even these smaller tasks take a long time and eventually exhaust me. In normal, everyday fatigue, the person who is exhausted, always has a small reserve of energy to draw on. In the kind of exhaustion that I am describing it feels as if there is no such reserve.

What is also clear to me now is that just as my physical behaviour is significantly affected by my going 'down', so is my cognitive functioning. For example, my memory for words and events, and my ability to make a clear argument, also deteriorate when I go 'down'. At that point, my self confidence decreases and so does my ability to be assertive. This is not an easy situation to manage! However, if I simply wait for the levodopa to work, I nearly always get back to 'almost normal' within about an hour and a quarter.

With all the symptoms that I have described above, one

would be excused for assuming that I am an unhappy person, full of despair at the progression of my Parkinson's. Yet, one only has to look at my daily experience from my own point of view to realize that I feel fortunate and that my days are usually rewarding. The key words in the last sentence are, 'from my own point of view'. We all see the world from different vantage points.

With regard to myself, I don't think that I can do better than to agree with Freud's description of the two factors which he said were basic to happiness. These were to have someone to love and to have something to do. Or, in other words, love and work; work and love. These two needs are definitely true of myself. If my close relationships are good and I have a project that enthuses and stimulates me then I am genuinely happy. It seems that so far I have been able to accommodate a gradually worsening Parkinson's into my life. This is not because I have a particularly unique temperament, although I do have a positive outlook. I feel that being positive keeps me open to new ways of helping myself, whereas if my outlook were negative I might not notice them.

The thing that keeps me going is a conviction that life is worth living, a recognition that it is short and that obstacles that place themselves in my way are potentially a waste of my time, so that I cannot bear to waste any more time in bemoaning them. Instead, these obstacles can be clambered over, burrowed through or crept under by using all kinds of ways and means. In the next chapters, I intend to describe some of the methods that I have used. I hope to keep the tone of this book at an appropriate level; not so negative that it disheartens people, nor so positive that it sickens them!

2
NEW FINDINGS AND A REDISCOVERY

My right arm has given me muscular pain for several years. When I go 'down' it starts shaking, tightens up and the more I shake the more it tenses. If I attempt to carry out any physical task when I am in this state the muscles in my right arm become more tense and rigid. Even mental tasks can cause the tension to increase. So, in these circumstances I move as little as possible and even think as little as possible.

Over the last two years or so, my other limbs have started to join in with my right arm, not so much in the sense of being painful but as regards shaking. The first one to join in was my left arm, then my right leg. Nowadays, my neck occasionally joins in as well, not that I am classifying it as a limb!

At one time, I was seeing different consultants every six months and one of these people, a retired neurologist with a particular self declared interest in Parkinson's, suggested that I ask my husband to stretch my right arm by pulling it, twice per day. He also suggested that I take up drinking black coffee. I was quite pleased about the latter suggestion although the former didn't fill me with much confidence. However, I was wrong; the arm pulling worked. If Jack pulled my arm or any other limb when it was tight and painful, the pain just drained away. (As for the black coffee, I have no idea if it is beneficial or not, but I enjoy it and I can claim medical advice as a justification for drinking it!)

Well, one thing led to another and I soon found out that when Jack shook my arm, after he had pulled it, that also made it feel better. Then he shook me by the shoulders and that helped too. So, now we had a routine for coping with tight, aching muscles: first of all we tried the arm or leg pull and then, by holding the shoulders, a gentle shake of the whole upper body. The shaking acted well, giving me freedom from muscle contractions within a second or two. It was as though, when I was shaken, my muscles were freed from a kind of relentless, locked rigidity and could once again relax. It reminded me a little of when a crumpled garment is shaken free of creases.

I continue to find these stretching and shaking methods extremely helpful whenever I am in muscular pain and I am describing them here in case they help anyone else. Mind you, they do surprise people. Embarrassed remarks are sometimes made about referrals to Social Services when Jack pulls my arm in company! I now occasionally ask other people to pull my arm, yet so far have not asked anyone to pull my leg! By the way, I find that the limb pulling and upper body shaking can be repeated several times during a bout of pain or discomfort. The pulling works well with pain in a particular limb, whereas the shaking helps me more when I have a sense of generally tightening up all over and feel more restricted in my movements than in pain.

I was well into this pulling and shaking mode in dealing with muscle contraction when I had a great surprise, which

I shall describe after a slight diversion into my life many years ago when I was teaching Psychology to adults. When I taught Psychology, I always ensured that I paired a session on statistics with one on Freud, (both subjects formed part of the syllabus.) This was because most of the adult students I taught were very nervous of anything resembling mathematics, but they definitely enjoyed hearing about Freud. They were particularly fascinated by the sexual elements of his theories. I knew that they would do well in the statistical parts of their examinations if they simply let me teach them statistics and if they carried out the statistical exercises which I set them. So, during each lecture, I unashamedly rewarded my students with accounts of Freud's life and thinking, after they had worked at their statistics. This method proved to be very successful. Hardly anyone failed the statistics aspect of the examination and they also answered the question on Freud very fully!

Whilst I was talking about Freud, I would tell my students about the time, during the eighteen eighties, when he worked for a year under the guidance of a renowned physician named Charcot, who worked at the Salpêtrière, a major hospital in Paris. Charcot specialized in treating patients with neurological conditions.

It was not until recently, nearly forty years after I was teaching these students, that I read that Charcot had included people with Parkinson's Disease in his regular clinics at the Salpêtrière. At that time Parkinson's had various other names such as the 'shaking palsy' or 'paralysis agitans'. I had not remembered that Charcot had treated people with Parkinson's. But, then of course, in the past I had had no reason to notice this fact.

Now, we come to the exciting part (for me, anyway!); the part when I realized that Jack and I had independently found out what Charcot had discovered so many years ago. Apparently, Charcot had noticed that when people with Parkinson's conditions had endured particularly rattling and shaking journeys on the way to the hospital, sometimes in carriages drawn by horses over cobbled streets, they seemed to have benefited from the shaking. When Charcot realized the possible connection between shaking and symptom relief for his Parkinson's patients he designed a vibrating chair and encouraged his patients to have timed sessions in the chair to help their symptoms. Then he died and his chair must have been forgotten.

I was extremely surprised when I read the above! The shaking method had been used before to treat Parkinson's and I had not known! I realized then that over the centuries people must have found all kinds of ways of ameliorating the symptoms of Parkinson's and so I might stumble across more of these. I decided to keep alert to any possibilities, even from the most bizarre sources.

In fact, I found it bizarre that a disorder which involves shaking for most people with Parkinson's should benefit from an approach which involves more shaking!

In France, I have been introduced to Shiatsu, a method of physical therapy which uses pulling, pushing and some shaking of the limbs. Again, I have found this very helpful in the same way that I have found the shaking and pulling by Jack so helpful. I understand that Shiatsu is based on Chinese medicine and I have also recently heard that the shaking part of the routine that Jack and I 'discovered' is given an important role in certain Eastern religions.

During the months of the year that I spend in France I have spoken to several French people who have Parkinson's about the support they receive from the French health system. As in the UK, six monthly appointments with a consultant seem to be the norm. Also, the medications used are very much the same as in the UK. The big difference that I have noticed between the methods used in South West France and in the UK, however, is in the use of 'Kiné', a form of physiotherapy. The word is pronounced 'kinny' and is short for 'Kinesiology' which is a way of applying knowledge about the ways in which the body moves, to all kinds of physical problems, including those which Parkinson's people encounter. I first heard of its use at the France Parkinson's support group meetings. Everyone I met there received 'Kiné' at least twice per week. At first I didn't pay much attention to this fact, assuming that I had no need of the treatment.

However, I have recently started to receive two sessions per week of Kiné in France and I have been told by the Kiné practitioner that the justification for this is to help retain fluidity of movement. One outcome of Parkinson's is that the patient can become locked in position. Although I was already technically aware of this, I have only just started to grasp the importance of viewing Parkinson's from this angle. I am starting to understand the danger that I might become physically rigid and 'stuck'. I can also see that being 'stuck' could apply itself to one's state of mind as much as to one's ability to move.

A friend who has suffered for much of her life with depression tells me that the physical symptoms of Parkinson's remind her of how she feels when she is going through a depression. For example, she may feel stooped and hunched. She can also feel locked into position and unable to move. One of my understandings of depression is that it can involve the depressed person treating themselves in an obsessively rigid, critical and cruel manner, readily blaming themselves for all kinds of weaknesses and offences. In effect, the spontaneously happy, fun-loving parts of the person become imprisoned. Such people can develop an intransigent refusal to allow themselves to look forward with hope. It seems to me that the two major illnesses of depression and Parkinson's Disease can inflict similar restrictions on their sufferers, for different reasons.

I am now using all the physical means mentioned previously to try to counterbalance the negative effects of Parkinson's on my movement. I hope that the pulling and shaking methods; the Shiatsu and the Kiné, including massage; will encourage my muscles to keep moving. As I understand my condition more, I am becoming aware that reversing the stultifying effect of Parkinson's on one's movement requires other people's intervention. I cannot cope on my own with Parkinson's restrictions on me and I welcome the people who are willing to pull me, shake me and generally insist that my muscles do not become locked and turned in on themselves.

My heart goes out to those who don't have anyone to help them in this way.

3
BEING IN PUBLIC

On the whole, the general public likes people to act predictably. People don't normally appreciate bizarreness in others. Children who show unusual behaviour at school are frequently bullied. Grown ups who act strangely are often excluded from everyday interactions with other people. (That is, unless they are wealthy; money changes things!)

The population expects people, particularly strangers, to act in ways that are expected of them. Manners help to smooth interactions between people. For example, if I accidentally tread on someone's toe, I will be expected to show some remorse. Behaviour that is unusual and surprising, confuses and even frightens the onlooker and, if he or she is not particularly experienced, they may shun or even persecute the individual who is acting in an unusual fashion. People such as the police, who view themselves as having a major role in keeping the public calm and compliant, may become agitated if they are faced with unpredictable persons.

Where does the Parkinson's person fit into this daily struggle for recognition and understanding? For a start, people with Parkinson's exhibit many unusual behaviours. For example: they may move very slowly; they may shuffle; their limbs may jerk and they may speak unclearly, even in a whisper. These are frequent, familiar symptoms in Parkinson's, but they are not familiar to the general population. So, a person acting in this manner is in danger of being ignored or, in some cases, mistreated by a public that doesn't understand.

As time has progressed since I was diagnosed with Parkinson's, it has become more evident that I am disabled. At first it was not so obvious to others and there was a period of time, over several years, when I was able to hide my condition. Now that I have had Parkinson's for about thirteen years since diagnosis, I appear disabled in public to a greater extent than before and I have tried to manage my feelings in this situation. When I go 'down' I shake a lot, stiffen up, stoop, can only move very slowly and generally look and sound incapable. I become embarrassed when this happens in public and it is tempting for me to withdraw as fast as possible! However, I have found some strategies that help me and I list them below. As I have emphasized before, just because these strategies work for me, doesn't mean that they will work for everyone else.

Suggestions about being in public...

1. As with all situations, I plan ahead. If I go 'down' in public I don't want to find that I've left my tablets, mobile 'phone, glasses, bottle of water or money at home and so my handbag is tidied and ready for the next outing, immediately after the previous one. (Having just written this I managed to lose all my credit cards! So much for sounding efficient...)

2. I avoid going out on my own. If I went 'down' badly, on my own in a public place, I would have many problems.

3. When I do go out I try to take someone's arm. This can be my husband's, a friend's or even, after explaining my situation, a new person's arm.

4. I put my 'bad side' next to my helper's arm. This applies when I am in the theatre, the cinema, a restaurant, the underground, a bus, etc… The reason for putting my 'bad' side near to the other person's arm is because this side is likely to shake. It could be very embarrassing if I found myself shaking vigorously next to someone I didn't know!

5. If I have to stand in public and don't have someone's arm to hold on to (for example, if my helper has had to leave me briefly, to go to the toilet or to buy tickets) then I search out something solid, like a wall, a door or a large piece of furniture and I lean against it with my 'bad' side. Sometimes it is enough for me just to hold onto something small, like a door handle. That way I gain a sense of physical stability.

6. Of course, supermarket shopping trolleys are absolutely invaluable for giving one an excuse for standing still when one has the need. (After all, if I do stand looking at the sardine cans for a while, who is to know that I do not have a passion for canned sardines?) Trolleys are also wonderful for leaning on and for holding onto, to try to control any shaking.

7. I don't take printed books out in public because I am very likely to shake when reading. I find that the print leaps up and down to such an extent that I can't keep track of the words.

8. However, e-books are very helpful; the size of print can be altered on an e-book and large print counteracts the jumping up and down phenomenon. These books can be of great help in waiting room situations.

9. I have not yet used a music pod or similar for listening to auditory books or music. Some Parkinson's people use music to help their rhythm when walking.

10. I try to day dream. A long time ago I discovered that if I day dream I do not shake. Although I cannot wish daydreams into existence, I can relax and hope that one will come to me. In this way a daydream does often start and if it does, I stop shaking. This particularly helps me when I am sitting on a seat in the underground. However, it would not work for me in the standing position. I would probably fall over!

11. Whenever I have the opportunity to listen to someone who interests me greatly or to observe someone who has a particular skill, I find that this calms my shaking. In other words, being absorbed in someone else or something else certainly helps.

12. If I get the opportunity to talk to a friendly stranger when I am out in public I do so and if my problems show because I am 'down' then I will say that I have Parkinson's. This usually provokes chat and I am very pleased if the other person seems interested in Parkinson's Disease.

The above list gives ways that I have found helpful in coping in public. However, many people with Parkinson's feel so embarrassed about meeting new people that they stay out of situations where they are likely to do so. This is a difficult problem to deal with and I have every sympathy. I often feel extremely ill at ease in public. The worst for me is when I have to stand and wait while the 'normal' people chat and I become more and more aware of my looking different, being physically uncomfortable and sometimes in pain. It is at a time like this, that I dread breaking into a shaking fit or a dyskinetic dance. Going through the whole rigmarole of shaking, becoming rigid, moving very slowly and having a tendency to fall over is much easier in the company of people who have PD than those who don't, because Parkinson's people 'understand'. I feel that it is necessary to help people without Parkinson's to 'understand' as well.

On several occasions recently, I have managed to feel less awkward in the presence of people whom I don't know and I have felt proud of myself when I have gone 'down', without embarrassment, in an unfamiliar situation. I was recently visiting a small art gallery in France when I suffered one of my Parkinson's 'attacks.' I found a comfortable couch to sit on, tried to relax and went through the usual shaking, muscular contractions and restricted movement routine on my own. I had reassured the group I was with that I would be all right and so they had gone off to inspect the art works. I was sitting near to the entrance and several people came into the gallery and looked at me, but I was not embarrassed. I felt very pleased with myself for what

Jack calls, 'looking odd with confidence' and rejoined my friends when I felt ready. However, I must emphasise that I am not able to show this kind of confident behaviour at all times.

Parkinson's is a complicated condition with many anomalies and contradictions. I am sure that some people with Parkinson's manage to live meaningful lives by avoiding the company of others. However, I feel that human relationships are so important that I would prefer to take the risk that some people may regard me as odd, rather than avoid meeting new people and taking part in mainstream life. My view is that loneliness, isolation and their consequences are worse than Parkinson's. So, whether embarrassed or not, I try not to avoid situations where I will meet people, new or familiar. I feel that it is of crucial importance for me to continue communicating with other people.

Post Script
Since writing this chapter, I have been thinking about how important my friends and acquaintances are in helping me adjust from being someone who used to live in their world but who now looks out at them from a kind of imaginary plastic bubble. Nowadays, I live in a restricted world but I can still generally associate with others as myself, the person I have always been, because my friends have been so generous in accepting the bubble that surrounds me and accommodating it in their world. I want to continue to socialize with others and the support that those close to me have provided, both in France and in England, has given me the confidence to make new friendships,

some of which are with people who have Parkinson's Disease. I was recently talking to a friend about my gratitude for the help that he and others had given me. He replied, 'it's because you make it easy for us, Terry.'

I thought about his remark and rang him to ask what he had meant by the word, 'it'. What was the 'it' that I had apparently made easy for others? He replied that 'it' was the elephant in the room, the subject that people do not usually discuss or ask questions about, for fear of causing upset. 'It' was my feelings about having Parkinson's. Because I talked freely about these feelings, other people did not feel embarrassed when the subject came up.

I was grateful to my friend for these words. But then the more I thought about my ready enthusiasm in talking about Parkinson's, the more I became painfully aware that my accounts of the condition could easily be boring some of my friends and acquaintances to death!

One of my French friends recently quoted the nineteenth century Prime Minister, Benjamin Disraeli to me, 'Never complain. Never explain.' She commented that in my writing I didn't complain, but that I explained in minute detail!

I hope that not too many people have found my attention to detail, heavy-going, but I thank them for persisting in their attempts to understand what it is like inside that plastic bubble.

4
CRISES

Suddenly my life took a plunge for the worse.

My 'downs' (Offs) became more extreme. The reasons were threefold, I think. The first reason was the faster wearing off of levodopa after having taken it long-term. This effect is well known and is to be expected.

I believe that the second reason was that a few months into our most recent stay in France I had to reduce my drugs intake a little because of shortage of money. The UK and France have an agreement that the British patient pays up front and then the French state pays the majority of this money back into the British person's bank account. As usual, I had paid up front for my medication and awaited the usual repayment by the state. However, over a period of several months this didn't happen and I was running short of the wherewithal to pay for my monthly medication order. Somehow, I had become involved in a long-winded bureaucratic process whereby I was given conflicting advice by various people. In France, it seems that many bureaucratic regulations are subject to interpretation by the worker in question and for every bureaucratic ruling there appears to be more than one way of understanding it and even more ways of putting it into practice.

The third reason, which I believe contributed to my problems was also to do with payment for one of my medications. I was shocked to find that a generic version of one of these was suddenly removed from the market and its place was taken by a branded drug which cost almost three quarters more. As I was still not being paid back for my normal drug requirements, I could not afford the gigantic increase in cost of the rebranded medication and so, again, I had to decrease the dose of the drug in question. Although I did discuss this with my consultant in England by e-mail and it was not a dangerous situation, nevertheless, I feel that having to cut down the intake of two of my Parkinson's drugs may well have contributed to my more difficult 'Off' periods.

(I have to digress here to express my thanks to the many French people who volunteered to help me. With customary French rebelliousness they offered to demonstrate in a nearby town, outside the administrative building which seemed to be the site of blockage of my money. People volunteered to make banners and install themselves outside the building, shouting suitable slogans. I knew that they were serious because at the beginning of our first stay in France, several years prior to this, Jack and I had been asked if we would join in a demonstration against a plan to use a picturesque local valley as a 'dump' for large amounts of waste. We had been equipped with appropriately worded T- shirts and loudly expressed our views in French about not wanting to live in a dustbin. (Jack later said that he wasn't too sure what he was expressing!) On that occasion we were demonstrating outside a regional government office. Barring our way and presumably defending the building were about six policemen, equipped with guns. They looked somewhat bored. After some more shouting, several speeches, tears and a lot of kissing we all dispersed. The atmosphere had been generally friendly, including the attitude of the police.)

In the case of my elusive money, a demonstration was eventually not needed. Someone in the village was able to talk to someone, who talked to someone else, who was able to un-block the blockage. Nevertheless, this all took over six months to resolve and did deprive me of some of my medication.

My 'Off' periods were now deteriorating to the point of being incapacitating.

The manifestations of these deeper 'downs' were periods of enhanced, uncontrollable shaking, an absolute inability to do any more than one thing at a time, (to the extent that I could not even do simple tidying whilst talking) and a fragile response to situations which required physical or mental effort. In fact, in these states of 'down', I could not tolerate carrying anything, even a piece of paper; I could not bear any physical pressure such as someone leaning on my arm; or any psychological pressure such as an argument; not even a voice that was too loud.

So, matters were not good and then they got even worse...

I had been having trouble with muscular contractions in my right arm for several years. Sometimes they would move to the left arm. But now I was developing back pain as well. It felt as though the muscles in my back were contracting. I saw an osteopath who thought that I might have a problem such as a trapped spinal nerve which could be being exacerbated by the Parkinson's contractions of my back muscles. We were shortly due to return to England and so it seemed unwise to complicate matters by starting any tests or treatment in France when it would be very likely that they couldn't be completed. Moving was becoming difficult and I had to hire a wheelchair. Shortly, the day for leaving France came round. We were to return to England by 'plane.

By now I was constantly in the wheelchair and my back and right leg hurt a lot. Our French friends took us to Toulouse airport early in the morning and I was delivered to the airport staff who dealt with disabled people. Jack was filtered off in another direction. Soon, I was joined by a lady who had broken her leg. We were both pushed in wheelchairs around the back area of the departure building to complete the necessary procedures before being moved towards the plane. I cannot praise the staff at Toulouse airport enough (nor those at Gatwick, when we arrived there.) They were all polite, knowledgeable, considerate and gentle. The person who had broken her leg and myself were then transferred into a passenger hoist and the hoist lifted us high into the air. We were to be transferred directly into the airplane, from the outside, through a door near to the captain's cockpit.

It was then that the hoist broke down...

I have often thought that I would enjoy writing an etiquette book with advice about how to behave when in unusual circumstances. I have been lucky to have experienced quite a few incongruous situations in my life and this one qualified itself as at least unusual. We were dangling in the cold morning air, high off the ground, and pointing directly into the captain's cockpit where the captain was having his breakfast and reading some papers. My companion with the broken leg and I stayed in this intrusive position for what felt like at least half an hour. Every so often the captain's eyes and ours would meet and both sides would try to compose appropriate expressions which would be suitable in this unusual and lengthening experience. Meanwhile, all the other passengers were still queuing up on the ground and were not able to get on the plane until the hoist was persuaded to start to work again. I gathered this information later from Jack.

When we eventually arrived back in the UK, I can honestly say that I was in agony. Luckily, we were initially going to stay with Judy and Mike, some friends who have a sound understanding of Parkinson's Disease. Mike has Parkinson's, and Judy and he seemed to have gathered together many of the mobility aids, specialized equipment and gadgets needed by the typical Parkinson's person. It felt like being in heaven, a Parkinson's heaven. I was so grateful to have been welcomed through the pearly gates, as I crawled up the stairs to our bedroom. Judy has since told me that I looked terrible!

5
SINKING AND RESURFACING

I was still not clear whether my leg and back pain were part of having Parkinson's or not. I managed to organize emergency appointments with my doctor and with my Parkinson's consultant and between them they arranged for me to have an MRI scan.

The scan revealed that I had a fractured vertebra. There, on the screen, could be seen the offending party. It was a vertebra called L4 (lumbar vertebra four, in the lower back region) and apparently L5 was not in good shape either. An objective fact had entered my unhappy world; I now knew the reason for my pain. How I had damaged the vertebra I had no idea, but I was told that fractures such as mine can happen without warning, often owing to the effect of age on the spine. It was advised that I see a back specialist, but there seemed little likelihood of this happening soon because, I was told, the waiting lists were very long.

I was given morphine to deaden the pain, as well as Co-codamol which contains codeine and paracetamol. I knew that these medications could be addictive. I was also told that they can cause constipation. Parkinson's Disease can encourage constipation, as can Parkinson's drugs and so this was a significant piece of information which, I later discovered, deserved to be taken very seriously.

My Parkinson's took a back seat, but like all back seat drivers it made its presence felt. For example, my careful routine about taking my Parkinson's medications fell to bits and predictably made things worse. Jack had to take over the organization of this task for a while.

I lost my self confidence. I was so overwhelmed by the pain that I couldn't remember things. I forgot that people had visited me. I couldn't plan. The pain increased whenever I moved. At the same time my Parkinson's symptoms became stronger, causing my arm and back muscles to contract and stiffen. When this rigidity occurred, it sabotaged all of my attempts to lie or sit comfortably.

Then I got stuck in the bath! Until the onset of the back pain, I had been positioning myself on all fours to get out of the bath. This method was now impossible for me, but I had temporarily forgotten the fact. So, when I tried to remove myself from the bath, excruciating pain stopped me. The ambulance people were called, but luckily my eldest son arrived before they did and Jack and Steven somehow managed to extract me from the bath with the help of towels to protect my modesty.

Pain was forcing me to live in the present. The past was eclipsed and I had no energizing impetus for making plans for the future. I have never believed that it is possible to live wholly in the present despite the fact that many wise people have advocated this. I feel that my memories of past experiences are part of the person I am now and, as regards the future, I derive great pleasure from making plans and envisaging new possibilities.

What I did most of the time was to cry and sleep. When I awoke I would try to focus my thoughts onto what I could do about this awful situation, but rapidly the pain blocked out any such effort. By now Jack was doing all the housework, shopping, seeing to the laundry and preparing meals, although I could only eat a little and in fact lost over a stone in a few weeks. (There are always compensations!) One of our friends regularly brought round home-made soup, to help us. Sometimes I could not wash myself and needed Jack to do so for me. I felt out of control of my life, especially because my ability to move had deteriorated so much. I became tearful whenever anything vaguely emotional was mentioned. In fact I cried a lot. I felt that I was an unfair burden on Jack. This was the lowest point I had reached since developing Parkinson's.

What eventually helped me turn the corner was something that Jack had often stated in connection with his work as a graphic designer. The phrase was, 'there is always a better way'. I tried to fit this idea to my situation as I lay in my sorry state, on the bed. There had to be a better way of coping with all this.

First, I dragged myself to the computer and looked up morphine. I found out that morphine has all sorts of side effects including causing the patient to cry. This was the second objective fact that had entered my highly emotional universe in a few weeks. During that time, whenever I had tried to explain what I was feeling or tried to get together some sort of plan with anyone, I would cry. But now I had learned a new fact: that a side effect of taking morphine was to encourage crying and so I realized that some of my many tears were caused by a chemical substance. This was not under my control and so I could do little about it. I drew comfort from this conclusion.

Suddenly, I was offered an appointment with a spine surgeon. We could not travel by underground to the hospital because of the pain I was in, and so Jack and I took a highly expensive taxi into central London. When we arrived at the hospital reception desk we were intrigued to hear someone say, 'It's like a mad-house upstairs'. We took the lift to the second floor, me in my wheelchair.

The waiting area outside the surgeon's door was too small for the number of waiting patients. This surgeon specialized in people with spinal difficulties and so it was not surprising that many of the patients were in wheel chairs. Wheel chairs take up extra space, but this fact did not seem to have been taken into account by the planners given the narrowness of the corridors. As a result, major logistical problems occurred whenever a patient in one wheel chair wanted to pass a patient in another wheel chair. Parking was another difficulty. Patients in wheelchairs were parked in every conceivable place including: small offices which led into the corridors, in a toilet with the door open, in a space outside the lift. The major challenge for the staff and patients who could walk, was to move themselves from one wheelchair traffic jam to another. Yet everyone seemed good-humored. I admired the patience and politeness of the British public.

I was reminded of a time, many years ago, when I spent my Christmas Day working with 'Crisis at Christmas'. After a thought provoking day, Christmas night came around. We were approximately ten volunteers and four hundred homeless people in a kind of church hall, as I recall. There were also a large number of mattresses. The final job that the volunteers had to do, at the end of the day, was to lay the mattresses onto the floor. The aim was to cover every inch of the floor, so as to give as many people as possible room to sleep. For a significant amount of time this challenge was our priority. We all worked intensively at the task and I felt a great sense of satisfaction when we had finally achieved a kind of jigsaw of mattresses filling the floor area. Each mattress was a temporary home for two people, for the night. There were not enough mattresses for one per person. There was also not enough room to provide a gangway of any kind between the mattresses. All throughout this time, those people who were homeless and who were waiting for their half mattress for the night showed no impatience, just as the hospital patients now seemed resigned to waiting their turn, in cramped conditions, in order to give the surgeon the space and freedom he needed to do his job.

As my reverie drifted away we were called into the surgeon's office and the contrast could not have been more surprising. Inside the surgeon's room all was peace and silent order. I felt that I was being admitted into another dimension where one could think, speculate and plan.

The surgeon apologized for the failings of the waiting area. Then he spoke calmly, confidently and knowledgeably about my fractured vertebra and various ways forward. We discussed the possible options. The first was to have one or more 'nerve root block' injections. These might help the healing process by reducing inflammation and there should be a reduction in pain. Then there were other steps that could be taken, including the option of surgery to the back. We agreed to start with a nerve root block injection.

Later that week the injection was carried out under a CT scanner whilst I lay on my stomach. I could feel the liquid seeping down, inside my right leg and radiating outwards throughout the leg. The pain was short but intense. I gathered from the doctor who had administered the injection that the procedure was rather hit and miss. Sometimes it worked well and sometimes it didn't. I was told to give it two to four weeks, to see if we had been lucky. Jack and I returned to our flat in another expensive taxi and I lay down yet again when we reached home.

I quickly realised that having another physical problem as well as Parkinson's produces a very complicated situation. In my case, the extreme, unpredictable pain in my back and my right leg was being made worse by my Parkinson's 'Off' periods. I could not win. Either it hurt me to move because of my back trouble, or I couldn't move as a result of the Parkinson's. As I learned later from my Parkinson's Consultant, it is not good for Parkinson's people to encounter additional challenges to their movement. Parkinson's attacks the initiation of movement and seems to take any opportunity to maximize this difficulty with the apparent aim of preventing one from walking again.

Whilst waiting for the nerve root block injection to work, I thought about my situation. I tried to list my problems in my head in order to think out ways of dealing with them. However, because of the continuing pain, I was not able to concentrate long enough to remember them. When I tried to write them down, my hand writing deteriorated faster than usual. Using the computer was painfully slow because I was shaking more than usual. I was behind with jobs such as paying bills, doing internet banking and generally organizing our living arrangements in England and France. Then, there was my writing about Parkinson's which had also been neglected. There were piles of paper for me to deal with and I did not have the physical strength to tackle them. The effort involved in moving pieces of paper, picking up pencils, finding files, turning the pages of books and looking in drawers and on shelves for the information I needed, was a major problem. By the time I had located a piece of paper and understood what needed to be done with it, I was too tired to complete the task.

Then I had a brain-wave. As I have mentioned before, I had long noticed that with the development of my Parkinson's, my ability to express myself in speech had paralleled my movement abilities. In other words, if I was 'down' and bumped into objects, not being able to walk in a straight line, then my ability to conduct an argument lost its direction and also became flawed. I would 'drop' words and phrases and my memory for words would fail me. My intellectual abilities mirrored my movement abilities. My inner world took on the characteristics of my outer world.

So, was it possible to do the opposite; to alter my inner world by changing my outer world? I decided to put this to the test.

6
SIMPLIFYING IN ORDER TO THINK

My idea was to make my external world as simple, straight forward and clear as possible, so that I could use it more successfully to think and plan. I felt hopeful that this would make me feel more positive. My recent back problem had disrupted what control I had over my life and had removed my self confidence about organizing myself.

Before I had Parkinson's I was able to grasp abstract ideas very quickly. I don't think that I am boasting; this was something which came easy to me. I also had a good memory and so I was readily able to make connections. In fact, when I was teaching psychology, I had great fun in connecting ideas from science with those about people and organizations. For example, the scientific concept of 'entropy' says that all systems tend towards chaos. I certainly agreed with that! I merely had to think of all the failed, 'new and revolutionary' systems of raising children, to realise that many ambitious plans end up in confusion.

But now my brain had changed and I needed to understand how to use it in the most useful way possible. From my many discussions with people who have Parkinson's, we agree that we can now carry out fewer actions at a time, compared with before we started the condition. This applies to physical actions such as washing up, as well as to actions that require much more thought, such as giving a point of view about a book or describing a holiday. It does not mean that people with Parkinson's don't have many ideas. It means that they find them very hard, or even impossible, to express or to carry out, given the need to focus on several things at once. Steadily diminishing energy compounds the difficulty.

For people with Parkinson's it is as if our ability to concentrate or focus on more than one thing at a time, steadily decreases. For example, in the past, when organizing a children's birthday party, I needed eyes in the back of my head, as well as several pairs of arms. I also needed to move almost automatically and to be aware of the different activities which the children were getting up to, at the same time as doing other jobs such as organizing the tea. (I usually got out of organizing the games!) In other words I needed, and had, the ability to focus on several situations at once. With Parkinson's this is no longer possible for me because the number of subjects or situations I can hold in mind at one time have substantially decreased in number. If I try to force myself I become exhausted. The reasons for this deterioration I leave to the experts.

So, it is understandable that a person with Parkinson's, who becomes less able to organize his or her life and becomes increasingly tired at trying to do so, can eventually become depressed at the apparent hopelessness of their task. This is where my emotions were heading after my back injury.

It was clear that I was now unable to focus on as many items as I had in the past. Jack and I agreed that I did not function well in situations where I was overloaded with information or had many options from which to choose.

In order that I might be able to think more clearly, the amount of information available to me had to be diminished. I had to have less possibilities to choose between and hence less likelihood of feeling overwhelmed by a large number of facts. We concluded that our first step down the road to achieving this, meant that we needed less things in our lives.

We live in two places; in France and in England. Both homes are small and hence, in order to further our aim of simplification, we did not have to down-size, but we certainly needed to off-load! This we did. We gave away a large amount of books. We only kept clothes that we could honestly say we used. We gave away pieces of furniture. We sorted through kitchen utensils, crockery and glasses, in search of things that were not necessary. We also got rid of many sentimental objects; photos, pictures and letters which at one time had been meaningful, but now were no longer so.

Professionals in France have told me that some people with Parkinson's become 'glued up', to the extent that not only can they no longer move freely, but they also lose the ability to distinguish between different parts of their bodies. I felt that change must be a counterbalance to this glued up state and that living in the past, emotionally, would oppose forward movement. I continue to feel that change is of great importance in stimulating people with Parkinson's.

Lastly, we ploughed through large quantities of paper work and threw a lot of it away. When I say 'we' did all the above, I mean that I suggested things to get rid of (and so did Jack), but he carried out the donkey work. My back was making much improvement, but I was now suffering a lot more from the good old Parkinson's characteristic lack of energy.

It was lucky that all this clearing out of objects was possible for us. However, if it had not been possible throughout our living area, I could have applied the same principles to a small area which I would have called my 'work space'.

Having completed our off-loading of material possessions, we turned to the bathroom to further simplify matters. I could no longer use the bath, not wanting to call out the ambulance service on a regular basis! The bathroom was a danger zone for me: towels to trip over; an inadequate shower, positioned over the bath; the possibilities of slipping. There were many reasons for me to call on Jack to help me in my ablutions, but I preferred not to ask for his help unless absolutely necessary, so that I didn't interrupt him unreasonably. We found a company that removed the bath, substituted a large walk-in shower for it and generally reorganized the bathroom, liberally putting in grab rails and making it much easier to use.

So, now we had a flat which was sparser in possessions, but richer in empty space. We had not yet simplified our French home, but we intended to do so at our next visit there.

Meanwhile, I had become more aware that I could now really do only one thing at a time. It seemed to me that I could now only deal with, or process, a single piece of information at once. So I set to, organizing my work according to this 'one thing at a time' principle. As already mentioned, my 'work' in the household is in the area of organization and communication such as doing the accounts, buying things over the internet, being the 'social secretary', planning and making meals and writing about my personal experience of Parkinson's.

I set up a system which I could use to access information, one piece at a time. I used a large number of plastic folders, file dividers, magazine organizers and ring-binders to tidy away and classify every piece of information I had. I was helped once per week for about six weeks in this major tidying and classifying task by a friend. No piles of papers were allowed any more. Every piece of information had to have a reason for being in the place it was put. There was an 'in tray' and a 'to do' tray, both labeled. The important effect of all this on me was that I could now really deal with one thing at a time, although obviously one file or ring binder actually held a lot more than one piece of information.

My new way of organizing my tasks gave me a feeling of being back in control of my life. Parkinson's has a habit of making one feel that one is losing one's power, and feeling powerless had not been good for my self esteem, but now I was back with a positive attitude towards Parkinson's, not in the sense of enjoying having the condition, but in the sense of taking up its challenges with enthusiasm. I could now think and plan and hope again!

7
ADVANCED 'UP' AND 'DOWN'

In the first book about my Parkinson's Disease, I described my 'On' and 'Off' symptoms, although I preferred to use the terms 'up' and 'down'. At that time I had had Parkinson's for about ten years. I have now had the condition for thirteen years and my 'up' symptoms are still very much the same as a few years ago, except that for most of the time I feel more unstable, in the sense of losing my balance and being in danger of falling over. I have to take care of this matter at all times. The fact that I do have 'up' periods is extremely cheering because they remind me of how it feels to be 'normal'.

My 'down' states have changed, however. This is what now happens, when I go 'Off' or 'down', as I call it:

Stage One

1. My right hand and arm start to shake a little.

2. Within about four minutes, the shaking increases significantly and continues for at least ten minutes.

3. If I am lucky the shaking gradually stops. This is, I suppose, because my dopamine levels have increased owing to the medication I have recently taken and so I have gone 'up' again. However, if I am not so lucky, I move on to Stage Two.

Stage Two

4. My muscles start to tighten. Usually this starts with the right arm biceps muscle and can sometimes spread to the left arm biceps. The muscles in my right forearm may then join in. Recently, other muscles have shown an interest in becoming involved. My shoulder muscles, my lower back and even my left foot have been the most recent to join in the fun. (I presume that this progression of my symptoms occurs because my dopamine levels, at that point, are still inadequate for my needs.) When the muscular contractions occur, I know that Parkinson's really means business. The contractions turn into rigidity and keep my shoulders bent and my head bowed. I cannot write, use an electric tooth brush or hold any object without great difficulty. I often drop things at this stage or I accidentally knock them over. My muscles cause me much discomfort and can sometimes be painful. I also have to guard against dribbling because, at this stage, I do not swallow saliva frequently enough. My speech becomes quieter and not as clear as before Stage Three began, presumably because my throat muscles become less efficient.

5. Walking becomes difficult because my general movement is restricted and uncomfortable. I need to sit down after short bouts of walking.

6. Going to the toilet (that is passing faeces) becomes very difficult. This is because the muscles in my

intestines slow down just as the other muscles that I have mentioned slow down. Constipation can then develop, which makes my symptoms worse and, I know, can cause other health problems.

Stage Three

7. Finally, I have a very surprising sensation which is difficult to describe and which has only recently become part of my 'On Off' routine. It is an increasing feeling of being unable to move. The effect on my personality is surprising to me; I don't panic but I know that I have to give in. Any effort is totally counterproductive. What I do is to try to relax and let another person or persons take over.

8. Eventually, after a time which can last up to about half an hour, but can be just for a few minutes, I start to move again. There does not seem to be any reason for this revival except for the fact that I have totally rested for a time. During this rest time I keep very still and try not to talk because talking is surprisingly tiring, as is listening. I also try not to think. If possible, I doze .

It has become evident that my new symptoms of being 'down' are not fully managed by my previous medications. The shaking is not particularly different, but the tightening and rigidity of my muscles has become far more insistent, uncomfortable and sometimes painful. The problems with movement, at Stage Three, are also manifesting themselves more frequently.

Parkinson's is a degenerative condition and so one has to expect that one's abilities will degenerate, but it is still a surprise when they do. I have found that the most upsetting feeling to me has been that of loss. We all know that we will die and most people accept this fact in different ways. We may even accept the possibility that we will degenerate on the way. However, because I have Parkinson's, I have had to face the reality of my slow loss of one ability after another from the moment I was diagnosed. Deterioration is loss and loss is poignant and saddening. Sometimes I have been tearful for a few days. I discussed this with my doctor and he said that he thought it was a consequence of not feeling well over a long period of time. I think that tears are also a natural response to loss.

8
THE OTHER SIDE OF THE COIN

Many of the losses I have experienced in life have eventually shown themselves to be times of wonderful new beginnings for me and that is one of the main reasons why I believe in being positive about having Parkinson's. I have learned through experience that many apparently negative situations will open doors for me that will lead to greater happiness.

Those of us who have Parkinson's are told that the best prognosis for someone with the condition is to have good general health and a positive outlook. Having a positive outlook indicates hope in the future and the belief that there can be meaning, even in situations where there appears to be nothing but confusion and negativity.

I can only speak about myself, admittedly, but having Parkinson's Disease has possibly put as much happiness my way as it has taken from me. These are some of the factors that have made me happy and which would not have happened, had I not had Parkinson's:

-   I retired from my formal career earlier than I would have done. (I loved my job, was quite a workaholic and was also loyal and so I would probably have continued working at my post for far longer than would have benefitted my personal development – and the development of others!)

- Leaving my formal post gave me the opportunity to try less formal, less conventional work, particularly giving talks.

- Giving talks helped me to realize how much I enjoyed 'performing' to large groups of people. I surprised myself in that I was able to make people laugh quite easily and so I started to build humour into my talks.

- Going to France, initially for a year, was a great adventure. I had not ever had a whole year away from work before and so the sense of freedom and potential new experiences was exhilarating.

- Making new, very good friends and many new acquaintances has happened to me far more frequently since having Parkinson's, than before.

- Writing a book has been an enjoyable experience in itself and then, to have positive feedback from readers, especially when I have been told that I have given a voice to other people's feelings, makes me feel very happy.

- Recently, I have noticed that my writing (in the sense of composing) has made some improvement. This has given me a real sense of hope in that having Parkinson's has not stopped me making progress.

- I have had the good fortune to have worked with two French women in the part of France where we live. They have helped me to translate the two books that Jack and I have published in the UK. We intend to publish these French translations as eBooks. One of the women worked with me on the first book and the other woman on the second book. I have really enjoyed these sessions and I think that my partners in translation have as well. Sometimes, as adults we forget the joys of playing. I can say that, as well as being intellectually challenging, these translating sessions have often taken on the feelings of play. For example, when searching for the 'right' word we have teased each other and made fun of each other's ideas. We have 'collapsed' in mock, exaggerated praise when a sentence has fallen into place. We have frequently finished a session in a tired but satisfied state. I have really loved these 'traductions'.

- I love the countryside in France, where we live during the warmer months. The views have become engraved on my mind and they stay with me during the times that we are in England. In contrast, I now love winter in London. This time of year in the Capital epitomizes for me the struggle between optimism and pessimism. The natural state of darkness, cold, rain, slush and gloom can be balanced, if one is lucky enough to have a place that one can call home, by the sense of relief at returning there, to its light and warmth and welcome.

- I find communicating with others even more satisfying, since having Parkinson's, than before. Perhaps because my infirmity is now so obvious, people are able to feel more at home with their weaknesses in my presence than in other, more competitive situations. I have found that if I can know and accept my weaknesses, they stand a chance of developing into strengths.

To summarise, I have found that if I can temporarily suspend the tendency to think in predictable, general terms about Parkinson's (for example, 'having an incurable illness is a tragedy') and can be quite honest with myself about what my feelings are at any time, then, having Parkinson's is certainly an unusual way of living one's life, but not necessarily, not always, an unhappy one!

Finally, I am quite aware that in this chapter I have focused on very different kinds of feelings from those in the previous chapter. I often find myself having ambivalent emotions about my Parkinson's condition.

9
A SHOCK

In chapters four, five and six I related that I broke a vertebra in my spine and how painful and depressing I found this experience. I was given a 'nerve root block' injection in my back to help with the healing process and, to my enormous relief, the injection worked. It took time to work and I continued to have pain in my lower back and right leg, but things were definitely improving! This was approximately five months after my back and leg pain had started.

The nights became easier. At the beginning, I would ferry myself to the toilet during the night in my wheelchair. After some weeks, I would push the wheelchair and finally, I managed to get to the toilet without wheelchair help.

The days became more varied. At first, Jack and I ventured out of our London flat with me in the wheelchair and Jack pushing it. I enjoyed these rides because of the opportunity to socialize with others and Jack also liked the exercise which was particularly demanding when pushing me up inclines, despite the fact that by now I had lost two stones in weight!

We live in a flat on the first floor. I would crawl up the stairs and come down on my bottom. Jack had to carry the wheel chair up and down the stairs and so we were very pleased at its lightness. My oldest son and his partner had kindly bought it for me and its weight had been a major criterion in its favour.

Jack and I would make our way to our local shops every day. I have often found pleasure in the most unexpected situations and this was one of them. Going up the road to our local group of shops became a regular experience and developed into a social activity, in that we got to know a lot of the shop-keepers. For example, Christine who owns a hair dressing business was extremely kind to me. She invited us to sit in her shop whenever I was passing by and my back was playing up. Christine is fun to visit; a welcoming person who cares about others and is an excellent listener. She is more psychologist than hair-dresser! Some people energize a person and others drain one dry. Christine is of the first variety. Then there were Mr Subhani and Mr Khurshid, the manager and tailor respectively, at our local dry-cleaners. They were always so kind, concerned, friendly and courteous. Visits to the Portuguese café with its friendly atmosphere and tasty, novel foods also became part of our routine. These regular outings to the local shops contributed to my recovery schedule and all the time I was gaining confidence that we would return to France. (I had worried that we would not be able to do so, because of my back problems.) I started to feel normal again! Well, relatively normal, given my Parkinson's!

I relinquished the wheel chair for increasing lengths of time and then bought a rollator. This was a very helpful contraption that I could push in front of me as I walked along. It had wheels, brakes and a very useful seat. After a period of time with the rollator, I started walking on my own.

However, despite my delight at walking again, a worry lurked in the background. Why had my vertebra broken? How could I be sure that it wouldn't happen again? To what extent was my back healing up? Also, my hip joints and the lower part of my back were sometimes causing me a lot of pain. What was this about?

All of a sudden, the word 'osteoporosis' started turning up. The spine specialist's report stated that, as I was not known to have osteoporosis, I should have a bone density assessment scan - a DEXA. I puzzled over this sentence. I didn't understand at first. I started to read around the area of osteoporosis and I was shocked.

I had no idea that, in the 'developed' countries around the world, there was a large and growing population of people with osteoporosis. I was even more shocked to discover that people with Parkinson's had a higher rate of osteoporosis than people without Parkinson's, to the extent that women with Parkinson's had a 91% chance of developing osteoporosis and the men had a 61% likelihood of doing so.* Also, I had no idea that the UK does not routinely screen women of a certain age and those at particular risk for osteoporosis, whereas many other countries do. I was horrified.

The prognosis for a person with Parkinson's and osteoporosis who breaks a major bone in their body, is bad. These people are often in extreme pain. Their bowel and bladder functions can pack up. They are immobile and in hospital. They are particularly vulnerable to infections, notably of the bladder.

What was particularly shocking for me was that I had worked with these people in the past, but had not realized who they were. Obviously, the individual people were different, but the problems which they suffered were the same. In my twenties, I regularly worked on geriatric wards as an auxiliary nurse, as a means of supporting my need to keep on studying. I also worked on many wards in psychiatric hospitals. I had, of course, not realized at that time that some of the patients that I met must have had Parkinson's Disease, some must have had osteoporosis and some both.

My experiences with the people I nursed on these wards were amongst the most heart-rending and uplifting of my life so far. I met with pain, death, indignity and courage on a nightly basis. (I worked at night for part of the week, so that I could study in the daytime.)

It was as a result of working on numerous wards, with people in various degrees of helplessness and suffering, that I evolved one of my basic principles of personal morality: 'Every human being has the right to be treated with dignity.'

I learned so much from my nursing experience. I came across many inspiring staff, but I also learned that cruelty can exist in situations where patients, who are particularly vulnerable, are in the hands of staff who dislike the work and who cannot come to terms with the immense questions of suffering and death that confront them regularly. But why and how did society expect these, usually untrained, staff members to cope through long nights on wards full of ill people, when feelings of pain and distress loom larger and are more frightening than in the comparative normality of the day? Although I feel that personal responsibility for bad behaviour cannot be ignored, I also feel that society has to face up to the responsibility of training people and paying them adequately for carrying out work on which many of us will one day depend to keep us alive and to maintain some quality of life. I hoped that there had been positive changes since my experiences, but realism made me wonder if that were so in this era of stringent cuts to public services.

And now, was I going to have to face such ordeals myself? Every part of me rebelled against that future. I felt let down by the system. Why on earth had I been allowed to experience Parkinson's for thirteen years without ever being told of the very high risk of developing osteoporosis and without giving me the opportunity of taking preventative action?

I felt even worse when I received the results of the DEXA scan. The diagnosis was osteoporosis in the spine and osteopenia (an early form of osteoporosis) in the hips.

Jack rang Parkinson's UK and described my situation. He asked if Parkinson's UK was doing anything to press the government about an urgent need for national screening for women and men that would provide early detection of osteoporosis, with particular attention for people with Parkinson's. Their response was helpful: firstly, they agreed that there was a lack of information about osteoporosis in the literature they provided; that they would put this right and they also said that, as a result of our query, they had now tabled various appropriate questions to be asked in parliament.

However, as I write this, over a year since our concerns were voiced to our local MP and to a member of the Tory government and questions were raised in Parliament, nothing has happened.

References:
* Invernizzi et al June 2009 in 'Parkinsonianism and related disorders'.

10
SURVEYING THE SCENE AND
A CHANGE OF FOCUS

For the best part of a year, I had been suffering all sorts of physical problems, in addition to Parkinson's, that had started when I had broken a vertebra.

Here is the sequence as I saw it:
1. I had osteoporosis (unknown to me);
2. So I broke a vertebra;
3. I was in great pain and so I was given morphine and Co-codamol;
4. As a result I developed acute constipation;
5. So I was given various medications to make me go to the toilet;
6. I then alternated between diarrhoea and constipation;
7. And I lost weight;
8. And I developed cystitis;
9. So I was put on antibiotics;
10. Constipation was still making me feel generally ill and I lost my appetite;
11. So I lost more weight, which made it about two stones in all.

In addition, my levodopa, taken as 'Stalevo', was not working as well as it used to and this was making my situation particularly difficult.

I discussed my concerns with my consultant who suggested that I have apomorphine injections which I would self-inject. I would be taught to do so by a specialist nurse. This should help me with my 'Off' or 'down' periods.

Apomorphine is a dopamine agonist that can be injected several times per day and is very effective for many people who have Parkinson's. (By the way, it has nothing to do with morphine.) Apomorphine is a 'rescue remedy'; that is, an anti-Parkinson's drug used to supplement levodopa when the levodopa has worn off or is not working properly. Hence people get extra 'On' time with apomorphine. The extra 'On' time can last for about ten to sixty minutes, depending on the individual. Apomorphine works quicker than other dopamine agonists because it goes straight into the blood stream. Before apomorphine was prescribed for me, however, I had to undergo a test in order to check whether I was likely to benefit from this medication. The test consisted of my coming off all my drugs for several hours, then being injected with apomorphine and finally, measuring the effect that it had on my Parkinson's symptoms. On the day of my apomorphine test, I had, as instructed, stopped all my medication since the previous night at two am. Then, I had left home at eight am and travelled by taxi for one and a half hours through a horrendous example of one of London's worst traffic-heavy mornings. By the time I reached the hospital I was shaking a lot and feeling ill. In the hospital I rapidly reached the point when I could no longer walk and was given a wheelchair. I also had diarrhoea pains and needed to visit the toilet. I had to have various tests, one of them being an electrocardiogram. As time went on I felt worse and worse and the medical people were starting to suggest that, because my electrocardiogram had been unclear (owing to my shaking), perhaps the apomorphine test should be cut short and continued in a few weeks' time. I leapt at this way out of the situation and was absolutely delighted to get home. For the twelve hours or so whilst I had been off my drugs I had felt dreadful. I sympathized greatly with drug addicts who have to endure 'cold turkey'. I find it almost impossible to describe how I felt, but if one can imagine a mixture of the feeling one gets just before fainting and that of wanting to expel diarrhoea, (but not being able to) then that approaches it.

The next day, I found that I had lost chunks of my memory. For example, one of my sons came in to ask me for some money that he had left with me. I had no recollection at all about his having left the money and for a while I was convinced that he had made a mistake. In fact, a few days later, I found the money, but still did not remember my son having given it to me. I was upset by this significant loss of memory because it felt as if a whole piece of my experience had been cut out from my consciousness, as if it had never happened.

My mind then said clearly to me, 'Enough's enough! Think!'

I thought carefully, for several weeks, about how I was managing my Parkinson's. Then, I turned down the offer that my consultant had proposed to me, of being taught to inject myself with apomorphine. Apomorphine might be very helpful for me at some time in the future, but this was just not the time for me to start using this medication.

The reason that I turned down the suggestion of self injection was because I felt that my body had experienced enough physical stress for the time being and now needed gentle treatment. However carefully I would be taught to self-inject, it would require strength in my hands to do so and I simply did not have that strength, especially when I was 'down'. (I knew that Jack would be very helpful, if needed, to carry out the injection task, but this would have meant that he would have had to be available at all times.) Also, people who inject themselves several times a day, regularly need to find new sites on their bodies to do so and my loss of two stones had reduced the surface area available to me! Finally, I had read that the regular self injection of apomorphine can sometimes cause little lumps on the skin which can become infected. I felt that I just did not have the energy to cope with all these potential new physical challenges and that, for the time being, I should continue taking my drugs in oral form only.

Now, I had to find a new way forward. I needed an alternative approach, a gentler, possibly more natural way of working with my Parkinson's, in addition to my medication. At this point I was having seven Stalevos per day and one Sinemet Plus for the night (this made a total of 800 mg of levodopa per 24 hours) plus two Pramipexoles per day (total 0.34 mg). I had been thinking a lot about what I called 'hard' and 'soft' medicine. 'Hard' medicine uses scientific thinking, in which scientific hypotheses are tested by experimentation and the outcomes carefully evaluated, often with the aid of statistical tests. The scientific approach to medicine has achieved almost miraculous results over the past two hundred years or so, examples being the virtual eradication of diseases such as leprosy and the control of polio and tuberculosis.

But other illnesses have been more resistant to such investigation, Parkinson's for one. A little thinking, however, suggested that some of the millions of people over the years who had suffered from Parkinson's must have found ways of dealing with their problems and living meaningful lives, in the absence of the medicines used today. The kinds of things I was contemplating were to do with nutrition, relaxation, meditation, hypnosis, yoga, exercise and any other approach I might stumble on. I called these methods 'soft' medicine. Other people might call them 'complementary' or 'natural' medicine. I was thinking about 'soft' medicine for clues that might maintain my hope of continuing to live side by side with Parkinson's. It still seemed to me that living as calmly as possible with this condition was more likely to be successful than fighting with it.

In addition to my Parkinson's, I now had the osteoporosis to consider. My first tactic, when I was diagnosed with Parkinson's, had been to learn about it and so I now learned about osteoporosis. I already had a vague idea that osteoporosis had something to do with a lack of calcium. However, I discovered that there was more than one theory about how the lack of calcium develops. The information given below is based on the theory that most convinced myself and Jack - a particular nutritional theory.*

According to this theory, the evidence is fairly clear that

56

osteoporosis is a rapidly developing disease in the Western, richer countries of the world, whereas in the poorer countries it is comparatively infrequent. The major difference between the richer and poorer countries is diet. Richer people eat far more meat and dairy foods than poorer people. Reduction of osteoporosis in the wealthier parts of the world might be achieved if the people who lived there consumed less animal protein and dairy products and more vegetables and fruit.

I learned that there are two different schools of thought about preventing osteoporosis: one is that we should ensure that we eat a good amount of dairy products and the other is that we should cut down significantly on animal fats and dairy products. I opted for the second recommendation.

The arguments that convinced me are, no doubt, open to all kinds of complex criticism, including from those with vested interests. But I did not have time for complexities. I urgently needed to try to cope with having osteoporosis.

I decided to change my diet, long term.

This was not as drastic as it seems because I had already made radical changes, three months earlier, as to what I was eating. My reasons at that time, had been to try to tackle the extreme constipation which I had developed. Constipation is a common problem in Parkinson's, but I had been lucky enough to avoid it until I had taken morphine a few months earlier for the pain that I was experiencing in my back and my leg. One of morphine's side effects is constipation. For those who have not experienced it, constipation may sound a bit of a joke and certainly not a 'problem'. But it can be a depressing issue and in my case it made me feel generally unhealthy and worked against my attempts to promote a feeling of well being in myself. So, I was very encouraged by the significant improvement that occurred when I ate a lot more fruit and vegetables and increased my water intake to just over a litre per day. Drinking through a straw helped. I found that, if I used a straw, I drank more liquid and I still find that this is true.

This treatment of my constipation was my first excursion into what I had decided to call 'soft' medicine. Instead of taking more chemical remedies to cure the constipation, I had altered some aspects of my life-style.

One of the reasons why I had not been drinking enough was because I tended to forget to do so. The obvious way of reminding myself was to write a note in my diary to that effect, but I had many other issues of which to remind myself and the diary rapidly filled up and a particular note was ignored.

I then tried sticking little amusing pictures around the place; pictures that said things such as, 'Have you done your exercises?' and 'Carry on Drinking'. However, like the diary, I tended to ignore the pictures after a while. I found that I had so many things to remind myself to do that I was always forgetting something. It was time for a new strategy to help me coordinate and remember my proposed 'soft' approach to Parkinson's and osteoporosis, as well as the more traditional approaches that I was using. It was then that The Chart was born!

References:
* Understanding, preventing and overcoming osteoporosis
  By Professor Jane Plant CBE and Gill Tidey
  2004 Virgin Books

  Osteoporosis How to prevent, treat and reverse it
  By Dr Marilyn Glenville PhD
  2010 Kyle Books

11
THE CHART

I originally thought up 'The Chart' in order to help me remember to take my medication on time. Since then the chart has been revised many times to cater for my other needs, but basically it is a list of the things I have to do to keep myself as healthy as possible.

I have always been a list-maker. I was born into a Forces family and over the years the call would suddenly come to move to another area of Britain or to go abroad. We had to bag up our possessions quickly, in endless numbers of cardboard boxes and I have vivid memories of my mother making lists of which possessions were in what boxes; counting them into the boxes in one place and then counting them out of the boxes in the new place, where we always had to learn new routines of living. Unfortunately we couldn't put our friends into the boxes and take them with us and so, learning new ways of living was often a lonely business.

People with Parkinson's have to learn new routines to try to cope with all the changes that occur in many of their physical and intellectual skills and they can feel quite alone when doing so. New routines mean new things to plan, remember and practise and it takes a lot of motivation for people to face up to the changes that are happening to them and to persist with their efforts to find ways of overcoming them. People need encouragement and, personally, I find it very encouraging to have my daily chart which gives me the impetus to remember my nutrition and drugs routines, as well as other matters, such as, 'Do your exercises!' I find it satisfying to tick off another job completed!

At present my chart is designed as follows:

Date:	After a small meal wait up to 1 hour before taking Levodopa. If a high protein meal wait longer before next Levodopa.					
Drug times	**Parkinson's**				**Dyski- nesias**	**Notes**
	Off @	**On @**	**Mins**	**1-4**	**1-3**	
1 **6.00** Stalevo Water						Alendronic acid MONDAYS ONLY before first Stalevo
2 **8.30** Stalevo Water						*Do leg exercises*
9.00 *Supplement*						
9.30 - 10.00 Breakfast+ **PROBIO+AGONIST**						
10.15 *Supplement*						
3 **11.00** Stalevo Water						
12.15 - 12.30 Snack+ *Vit D*+ *Supplement*						
4 **1.30** Stalevo Water						
1.45 - 2.15 REST+ *Supplement*						
2.45 - 3.00 Snack+ *Supplement*+ **AGONIST**						
5 **4.00** Stalevo Water						
5.20 - 5.40 Protein dinner- small						
6 **7.10** Stalevo **AGONIST**						
8.10 Dessert+ *Supplement*						
7 **9.40** Stalevo Water						
10.40 - 10.50 Late Snack						
Optional night-time Sinemet						
Total Mins	✕	✕		✕		

EXPLANATORY POINTS ABOUT THE CHART

- Each chart lasts for one day only, covering 18 hours from 6 am until midnight
- It states the times to take medications.
- Meal times and snack times are also given.
- There are places to fill in times of when I go 'Off' and then 'On' again, throughout the day. (In that way I can easily see for how long each 'Off' lasts).

Date: *dd/mm/yy*	Parkinson's			Dyski-nésias	Notes
Drug times *After a small meal wait up to 1 hour before taking Levodopa. If a high protein meal wait longer before next Levodopa.*	Off @	On @	Mins 1-4	1-3	
1 **6.00** Stalevo ✓ Water					Alendronic acid MONDAYS ONLY before first Stalevo
2 **8.30** Stalevo ✓ Water					*Do leg exercises*
9.00 *Supplement* ✓					
9.30 - 10.00 Breakfast+ **PROBIO+AGONIST** ✓					*Fruit breakfast + 3 pieces of toast (I was hungry!)*
10.15 *Supplement* ✓	*10.45*				
3 **11.00** Stalevo ✓ Water	*11.30*	45	3		*Bad down. Probably the toast*

- The severity of every 'Off' or 'down' is measured on a scale from 1 to 4 according to how difficult it is for me. One means not very difficult and Four means very difficult indeed.
- If anything of particular significance happens throughout the day, this can be recorded in the Notes column.
- The chart can remind me of specific changes I intend to make in my routine, for example, increasing Rest times.

- The chart can be altered at any time when this seems necessary. In other words it is definitely **not** set in stone. It is a working document.

As a reminder, what works for me does not necessarily work for others.

Using my chart helps me not to sink into doom and gloom whenever Parkinson's makes its presence felt. For example, it helps me to be more objective about how many 'Offs' I have per day and how severe they are. However, there is one golden rule I have to follow...

I have to fill in my chart regularly!

12
NUTRITION AND LEVODOPA

One of the ways in which I have used my chart has been to try to improve my response to levodopa.

People who have Parkinson's Disease lack dopamine, a substance which is vitally important in facilitating movement. Dopamine is produced naturally in the body from another substance called levodopa.

But levodopa can also be made in the laboratory, taken into the body via the mouth, then into the stomach, into the bloodstream and transported to the brain, where it can be made into dopamine. That is what happens in theory.

In practice, the artificially produced levodopa usually works very well for five to six years. However, after five to six years of taking levodopa, it does not work smoothly any longer and the Parkinson's person may develop further problems in all areas of movement.

At this point, I wish to thank Lucille Leader for the very valuable information that I have gained from several books written by her and her husband, Dr Geoffrey Leader. I have given the names of two of their books, the publishers and the ISBN numbers at the end of this chapter. I first read a book by Lucille Leader and her husband about six years after I was diagnosed with Parkinson's. I had just started taking levodopa and had been having a lot of difficulty with this medication. The nutritional advice I received from the Leaders' book helped me to function well with levodopa for six or seven years more.

Then, after about twelve years with Parkinson's, things changed again. My levodopa became less effective and several times per day I was having severe 'Offs' or 'downs'. I wanted to find some way of improving how the levodopa worked on me.

I decided to use my chart to help me observe how I responded to different foods and to the length of time I needed to digest them before taking levodopa. I tried all sorts of food combinations and recorded my reactions to these. I also noted my reactions to taking levodopa at different time intervals before and after meals.

By that time, I was very familiar with the effects that my drugs had on me. Hence, I recognized when the drugs 'worked' and when they didn't 'work'.

(At this point, I want to explain something about the progression of the 'On'/'Off' effect in myself over the years. Basically, I have continued to feel fairly normal when the levodopa is working well and I am 'On'. However, I am also regularly 'Off'. 'Off' means that the levodopa is not working properly or perhaps not at all. 'Off' has become more uncomfortable and painful for me. At present (thirteen years after diagnosis), these pains relate particularly to muscular contraction.).

With reference to the most recent recording of my 'Offs', on my Chart, I noted the times they started and finished and the time that the 'Off' lasted, in minutes. I also rated the severity of each 'Off' as shown in the scale below.

Severity of 'Off' or 'down'

Stage One	Shaking starts. Mobility good. Can write.
Stage Two	Muscles start to contract.
Stage Three	Muscle contractions increase. Mobility decreases. Start to feel discomfort.
Stage Four	Mobility very poor. Cannot write. Muscle contractions increase further. Start to feel pain.

This scale was to a large extent subjective, but there was also a factual element to it that depended on looking at my hand writing. At number Four, on the scale, I could not write at all, whereas at number One I had no problem with writing.

After having carried out these observations on myself for one to two months my conclusions were as follows and are still so, at the time of writing :

1. I have fewer and less severe 'downs' when I eat small meals more frequently, rather than large meals less frequently. Hence, I now eat small meals and snacks approximately five to six times per day, rather than the two large meals and the rather skimpy breakfast that I used to eat.

2. Eating animal proteins such as fish and meat were causing my 'downs' to be very uncomfortable and

sometimes painful. I found that a meal that included a substantial portion of animal protein completely stopped the levodopa from working on me. So, I cut down a little on eating these foods, but my problems continued. Then I progressively ate less and less of them until now I am almost vegetarian. I have tried to compensate for this by eating high protein alternatives, such as avocados.

3. I need to wait up to an hour, after a small meal, before taking levodopa. Needless to say, eating large meals is now out of the question for me!

4. Tiredness and stress affect the efficiency of the levodopa. I have made my life as stress-free as possible. I now have a rest in the afternoons when I generally fall asleep. It is necessary for me to drink plenty of water; one, to one and a half litres per day. This regulates any constipation.

I have always believed that it is of utmost importance to be self-aware, both physically and psychologically and 'The Chart' is one of my attempts to remain aware of the progress of my Parkinson's so that I may make the best use of new ideas as they come along.

My daily chart initially dealt only with Parkinson's Disease. However, when we discovered that I also had osteoporosis, Jack and I decided that the best thing I could do was to follow the nutritional advice we gained from reading around the subject of Osteoporosis.

(As a reminder, I had discovered that there were two main

hypotheses or explanations for why people develop osteoporosis. Basically, the first theory is that the lack of calcium in the body, which accompanies osteoporosis, should be treated by increasing one's dairy food intake. The other theory is that osteoporosis is caused by eating too many dairy products and animal fats and so the remedy lies in decreasing this type of food. I was convinced by the second argument, but I am not in any way attempting to convince others, although I would advise everybody with Parkinson's to learn as much as possible about osteoporosis.)

Luckily, the regime that I am following with regard to osteoporosis does not contradict the nutritional programme that I am following for Parkinson's.

Parkinson's Disease
   Reducing Symptoms with nutrition and drugs
   Denor Press Limited   ISBN - 13:978-0-9526056-4-5
Parkinson's Disease
   The New Nutritional Handbook
   Denor Press Limited   ISBN - 0 9526056 1 9

13
HUMOUR AND SADNESS

I was shaking a little as I entered the carriage. The medication was wearing off and I hoped that the tremor would not increase too much. It was rush hour on the underground and there was no available seat. So, I held onto the nearest support rail, grateful that Jack was with me. The trembling was becoming more noticeable and a lady got up and offered me her seat. I thanked her and sank down with relief.

"You got Parkinson's?" she asked.

"Yes," I said.

"My mother had Parkinson's," said the lady.

"Oh," I replied.

"Yes," said the lady. "She choked to death."

On hearing this woman's shocking announcement, I had a desperate wish to laugh. I could imagine that there were others within earshot also struggling not to laugh. It was not that the words were not tragic; they were. However, the context in which they were being imparted was all wrong, as was the fact that they were being addressed to me, someone with Parkinson's.

I have a similar reaction when I hear some of the words used to describe my Parkinson's Disease. Words such as: 'neurodegenerative', 'no cure', 'will steadily get worse' are so negative that my personality rebels on hearing them and I get an irresistible desire to laugh or to make quips such as, 'what's the bad news then?'

I suppose the above shows that one of my ways of dealing with the sadness of Parkinson's Disease has been with humour. For me, humour is a way of fighting back, refusing to give in. Sometimes it feels like the only way of doing so. Humour has a way of throwing everything up in the air and when it all floats back down and settles, there is a lessening of tension, a fresh way of seeing things, a new perspective. People benefit from smiling; giggling is even better, but a full-on laugh that takes up the whole being, is best.

Laughing out loud is often a response to farce; the aspect of humour that notes the ridiculous, particularly in quite tragic situations and can throw up funny comments in response. For example, I was being given a medical test on one occasion when the person in charge asked if I would mind not shaking for a few minutes, whilst the test was being carried out! I was lost for words, but if I had not been, I would have pointed out that I could be a millionaire if I possessed such a skill!

I have noticed that funny people do not seem to lose their sense of humour even if other abilities decrease. I have recently met a man, with at least moderate Parkinson's, whose skill in cracking jokes at a very fast rate is impressive. His ability to sum up a situation, to be aware of all sorts of ways of responding to it and then to select and deliver the most appropriate funny remark, seems to me to be extremely sophisticated. Parkinson's has not taken that away from him. I rang him to ask his permission to write the above and I was laughing as I asked him. He said, "don't laugh; I haven't made the joke yet!"

Well…. Some people don't have to, do they!

So far, I have avoided being depressed, but I am quite aware that this state of affairs (like my constipation!) could change. Parkinson's encourages depression in a number of ways: Firstly, there is the stark truth that this is a condition where change usually means that one is getting worse. Also, Parkinson's is described as being degenerative and as having no cure. Such a description does not exactly cheer one up. Next, the condition involves loss after loss after loss. For example, an early loss may be of being able to express oneself clearly in a discussion. Then there may be the loss of the ability to pronounce words clearly and to speak loudly enough to be understood. In a totally different area, there is the loss of flexibility of limbs and the loss of flexibility of inner muscles such as those of the gastro-intestinal tract, including those used for swallowing. Depression can start when a person feels out of control, that nothing they do will make a difference. Perhaps the saddest aspect of Parkinson's is that it happens slowly, inevitably and inexorably and can seem like the movement of a giant steam roller, slowly crushing one's life and plans.

Parkinson's persons have a tendency towards depression and anxiety. Whether this is caused by chemical changes in the brain, the problems associated with having Parkinson's or other reasons would have to be explored with each Parkinson's person separately. It is not in the least surprising that they become sad and depressed. However, help is available, although it often needs to be pursued a little. I mean that, although depression can often be managed with drugs and therapy, every therapist and every kind of drug therapy is not suitable for everyone. One has to put in some work to find the right person and method.

Sadness, however, requires a lighter touch. Humour is one way of distracting oneself from sadness, of detaching oneself. It can be a very powerful tool when used wryly, poking fun at a difficult situation. But sadness does not always have to be fended off. Sadness can be faced. When I am sad and I don't know why, I often use the following approach:

1. I write down or tell someone else (this has to be a loyal friend who is a good listener) all the reasons that might be causing the sadness, even the reasons that sound 'silly'. In fact, the silly reasons are likely to be the true ones.

2. From experience, I know that whatever is upsetting me at the moment is likely to have been triggered off by something that has recently happened. It is also very likely that my reason for being sad is as a result of someone else's action or inaction towards me.

3. I then write down or state what I have deduced is the reason for my sadness.

4. I try to respect my feelings enough not to dismiss what has upset me as 'ridiculous', 'childish' etc…

5. Now that I am clear what is upsetting me and can readily put it into words, I let myself think about this

particular sadness. I may cry and that is likely to help me because, after crying, I often feel as though I have put down a heavy burden for a while.

6. If my sadness is to do with someone else's remarks or behaviour towards me or about me, I decide what I want to do about the situation. This includes the option of doing nothing. I have found that consciously deciding to do nothing about a situation is quite different from doing nothing out of fear or laziness. Quite often I will draw up a plan, but will not carry it out straight away, if at all.

I have met several people with Parkinson's who have been treated in a very insensitive manner by others and who have been hurt as a result, although sometimes they can also see the funny side of these incidents. For example, when one of my friends was diagnosed with Parkinson's, she told someone else who said, 'you know that it will get worse, don't you?' Despite my friend's assurances that she was painfully aware of this fact, the person in question said the same kind of thing on several occasions, until my friend angrily asked her to stop. The 'insensitive' person then appeared hurt! Presumably she had been unaware of her need to upset my friend. The humour in this situation is, I think, tied up with shock at the lack of insight and empathy of some people, together with their bad taste!

Mind you, if I look back over my life, I still cringe at some of the remarks I have made…!

Insensitivity is not the prerogative of others!

14
TOUCH

Nothing has surprised me more, in the past few years, than the importance of the touch of others in helping me to cope with the progress of my condition.

It started as a result of my lumbar vertebra fracture (see Chapter Five). At that time, I was in considerable pain and was given morphine and Co-codamol to help me. I had several kinds of pain in my right leg. One of the worst was a feeling that my leg was being sliced with a bread-knife. At first, this pain occurred regularly and one day Jack traced his finger, very lightly, along the outside of my painful leg, from ankle to hip. I had an instant reduction of the pain. I asked Jack to do it again and it worked again. I felt elated.

After that, whenever I had bad pain in my leg, I would ask Jack to touch it in the way indicated above. He would draw an imaginary line along my painful limb from where I felt the pain, upwards (towards my head). Then he would start again and repeat the movement. This process did not work with me if he drew the line downwards (away from my head). Also, the touch had to be very light, almost imperceptible.

At a follow up appointment with the spine surgeon's assistant, I told her about the way that Jack was able to lessen and sometimes to remove my pain. I had wondered if she would understand what I was talking about, but she showed no surprise and readily answered. She explained that my pain was like 'phantom limb' pain. (When someone loses a limb they can continue to feel pain in the absent limb.) Similarly, my leg hurt even though the leg itself had not been damaged. The damage was actually in the area of my broken vertebra. She explained that Jack, by using a very light touch, was introducing confusion into my brain and as a result the pain was lessened.

Time passed and my leg pain eventually disappeared. Then a completely different but familiar sensation started to become worse. I mentioned in chapter seven that during my 'Off'' times some of my muscles had started to hurt. Well, over the months these muscles continued to contract regularly until they became very painful at times. The contractions occurred in the following muscles, when my medication was wearing off or had not started to work. Thankfully, they did not all contract at the same time!

1. Contraction of right biceps.

2. Painful left forearm. I found this quite strange because I was sure that my left biceps was doing the contracting but the pain was felt in the left forearm.

3. My shoulder and upper back muscles would contract on either or both sides.

4. My lower back muscles would contract on either or both sides.

The pain was specific to the particular areas I have mentioned above. When my lower back was hurting I could hardly walk and had to have frequent rests. However, if I asked Jack to hold his hand on the painful area for about twenty seconds at a time, then the pain would either lessen or go away altogether. I found this quite amazing.

I thought about how my Parkinson's was being managed. I was very satisfied with the traditional medical support that I was receiving in the UK. I was working collaboratively with my General Practitioner and my Consultant and I enjoyed my meetings with them, which were six monthly in the case of the Consultant and as necessary with the General Practitioner. When I was in France I had an excellent doctor, also. However, I felt that I should be helping myself further, searching for alternative approaches to my back pain and my Parkinson's. I kept coming back to the thought that people must have been suffering from Parkinson's for a long period before levodopa was produced commercially. What methods of lessening the symptoms did people use before levodopa?

At this point I met several people who mentioned the term 'kinesiology' to me. One was a long-standing friend who had recently become a student of kinesiology; another was an osteopath in France and the third person was a professional kinesiologist whom I also met in France. None of these people appeared at all surprised when I told them about the effects of Jack's touches, described above. They seemed to accept that this was quite normal.

Then I met with someone to whom I decided to refer myself for a treatment called KORE. This is an approach to physical and mental health that reminded me of aspects of what I had been told about kinesiology. For a while I had been looking for some kind of complementary therapy and this seemed to be right for me. Amongst my reasons for choosing KORE were that I liked Lucy who was the manager of the practice and the chief KORE therapist. My other reasons were that the practice was easy for me to get to, being very near to my home and Lucy described herself as having had a lot of experience with treating back pain.

I learned that KORE was a relatively recently developed therapy. It was devised by Dr John Brazier, approximately twenty five years ago. I was told that KORE had its origins in Chinese medicine and combines ideas about Western and Eastern medicine. Chinese medicine explains illness in terms of 'blockages' in the body. When the 'vital life force' is blocked, illness develops. Western medicine, however, concentrates itself more on symptoms and the particular indications they provide to a specific illness.

Eastern medicine focuses on the whole human being; physical, emotional and spiritual and is more concerned with helping the person to become stronger and more capable of dealing with life's crises than with identifying the particular disease that the patient may have contracted. Western medicine, on the other hand, focuses on the symptoms of the illness and sees its functions in terms of finding medication or other treatments to cure these symptoms.

Hence, Western medicine concentrates on medication that will remove the illness and its symptoms whilst Eastern medicine concentrates on strengthening the individual to give them the wherewithal to resist illness.

Initially, I booked myself in for six sessions of KORE. The

first session was wonderful. I lay on a comfortable, warm, professional looking divan that could be moved up and down. I lay flat and relaxed whilst Lucy did all sorts of things to various parts of my body and pulled gently at my legs and neck. All this lasted for about an hour. I felt utterly relaxed at the end of the session and then was exhausted for the rest of the afternoon. The next day I was still tired, but I was also exhilarated and felt that I was on the right road. I had this therapy once per week for six weeks and found it very helpful as regards my general well-being as well as for my back which felt more relaxed and I stood up straighter than before.

I feel that both approaches to medicine have their place and that I am very lucky to be able to access the Eastern as well as the Western way of medicine. Because Parkinson's is not curable at present, those of us who have the condition have to use every help we can get.

15
WHAT I KNOW

First of all, I would like to admit that I don't know a tremendous amount! However, what I do know I'd like to communicate to others in case any of it is useful.

I am not referring to knowing lists of facts and I am certainly not talking about using facts in order to impress. I am talking about the lessons that living has taught me.

For me, to really know something; to be so sure of it that I rely on this knowledge to support me, even in situations where I do not have support from other people, demands my actual experience of it.

1. The first thing I know is that hope and perseverance work. This statement sounds so boringly obvious that it runs the risk of being ignored. Nevertheless it has been true for me.
    (Please note that this applies to long-term aims. I am not talking about peeling a potato or cleaning one's teeth. In those cases a different approach to the problem is needed.)

2. I know that out of nothing comes something. By that, I mean that if I feel totally bereft and empty and if I just wait, some positive thought or transformation of my sad thoughts into an alternative way of perceiving the situation will occur and I will know what direction to take next. Hence,

it is very important that I deliberately build time into my life to do nothing and, as far as possible, to think nothing, so as to be able to listen to myself.

3. I know that I must face difficulties. If I do not face the difficulty and try to ignore it, then its shadow will loom larger and larger, affecting more and more areas of my life.

4. I know that it is not **necessarily** better to take action about a problem than to do nothing about it.

5. I know that it is very important for me to experience my sadness and not to try to avoid it.

6. I know that I have a day-to-day self and a wiser self.

7. I know that looking very carefully at a situation changes parts of the situation.

8. When Jack was a child his Auntie Enid said to him, on several occasions, that he should remember that no one was better than he was. I know that everyone deserves to have an Auntie Enid.

9. I know that just because a beneficial act has been carried out, for selfish reasons, this does not negate the beneficial action.

10. I know that one has to have a 'killer instinct' to do a job well, particularly if the job has to do with helping or protecting vulnerable people. By using the term 'killer instinct', this is my way of describing the kind of effort that is generally reserved for close members of a family or very good

friends. 'Killer instinct' means being unwilling to leave any stone unturned in the effort to work for the good of someone who is in a difficult, vulnerable position. Doing a proper job requires more than working for money.

11. I know that there is a positive side to feeling depressed: if one is very unhappy about one's situation and if the cause of this unhappiness can be identified, then, so long as the person concerned is not severely, clinically depressed, a plan can be made for change and that change can be achieved.

12. I know that if I want to change something important in my life, I can do so. This depends on my knowing clearly what I want to change and being able to put this into plain words. Then it depends on my being able to focus clearly and regularly on what I want to change, in order for it to happen.

13. I know that my wealth is other people.

14. I know that sometimes 'good enough' is great!

16
WHAT HELPS ME WHEN I GO 'DOWN' OR 'OFF'

I have given an account of my current experience of going 'down' or 'Off' in Chapter Seven of this book and then I have added to the account in Chapter Twelve. Going 'down' happens because the body is lacking dopamine and currently I go 'down' two to six times per day. As the years have progressed, my experience of going 'down' has become more difficult, but I have found that it can usually be made acceptable. I have listed below some methods that I have used to help myself in the 'down' or 'Off' situation. In most cases they involve other people. I have found that other people, even though they frequently do not realise it, have the ability to make my 'Off' periods much easier or more difficult to experience.

My 'Off' now starts with a few minutes of shaking. I have called this **Stage One**. (See Chapter Seven). This is not painful, but does make me feel generally very physically unsteady, heavy and lacking in energy. When I become aware that this 'down' is not going away for a while, I tell Jack or whoever is with me and we search out a seat or someone will often vacate one for me. The main problem with this stage is needing to sit down and so, if a walk is planned, the availability of seats has to be borne in mind.

The sign that I have moved to **Stage Two** is when my muscles start to contract. This usually starts with my right biceps and I sometimes begin to look pale and unwell. If the muscles in my back tense up very tightly I cannot stand without support. So, by this time, I give the opposite impression of someone who is a capable human being and I definitely look as though I need help! Every aspect of my movement is affected and my whole body just wants to sit down. If this situation occurs when I am at home there is no problem, but if I am out of doors then I have to find a place where I can sit and recover.

I welcome help from others and express my thanks when it is offered. Some people ask directly if they can help. Other people are worried about 'intruding', but an offer of help from a stranger has never given me the feeling that I am being intruded upon. I travel with Jack on the Underground quite a bit and I find that people of all backgrounds regularly offer me their seats, even when I am showing very mild symptoms. (Of course, it may only be me whose judgment is that the symptoms seem mild!)

I experienced great generosity recently on Paddington station. The 'disabled' toilet was not functioning. I was in one of my 'down' states and didn't feel safe in walking down the stone steps to the public toilets. Jack and I were discussing what to do when a woman came up and asked if there was anything she could do to help. I asked her if she would take me to the toilet. On the way back, she told me that she had a friend back home, in Australia, who had Parkinson's and so she had recognized my dilemma. I was very grateful to her and am similarly very grateful to anyone who 'intrudes' in my life in this way.

If I am in company and I need help, I may ask someone if

they would, for example, stretch my arm or shake me. However, I do not want to embarrass people and I feel far more confident in making such requests, if the people concerned are used to me!

If my 'Off' proceeds to **Stage Three**, this is when I really appreciate help from other people. At this stage, some or all of the muscles that I have mentioned, contract and I am in pain. By now I am not able to move easily and I feel as though I have hardly any energy. My speech becomes quiet and indistinct and I am very reliant on others. Here are some of the ways that people can help me.

1. Ask me if I take medication and how often.

2. Ask when I last took this medication.

3. Ask when the next one is due.

4. Asking these questions is very helpful for me because they remind me for how long the 'down' period is likely to last. It usually lasts over half an hour. Knowing how long I will be 'down' motivates me to hang on in there. For those to whom it applies, this situation can be compared to that of a woman who is in labour; it very much helps the woman to know how long each contraction is going to last.

5. Gentle conversation helps me sometimes; nothing where I have to answer complex questions, but reassuring talk on mundane matters is much appreciated at this point.

6. Some sympathy is also welcome. I find it very difficult to be told something to the effect that, 'You just sit there and we'll let you get over it! Tell us when you're feeling better'. If anyone says this kind of thing to me, I have evil thoughts!
(Having re-read this point I want to emphasise that I do not mean that I need constant sympathetic remarks. I simply want to be included in the group even though I may be in physical discomfort. Some one who had a brain tumour once told me how unhappy they had felt when pushed into a corner and left there on their own during Christmas dinner. The person felt ostracised and hurt. It is that kind of behaviour to which I am alluding here.)

7. At some point during my 'down' I feel that I can walk again and then I find it useful to walk around slowly. Even better, is to be walked by someone else who holds my hands, slightly higher than my shoulders.

8. As I start to emerge from a 'down', I appreciate gentle shaking of my shoulders and arms and even some rubbing of my feet to encourage me to move more freely. (These are not the kinds of things I would expect from a stranger!)

9. At the same time I exercise my legs by walking with exaggeratedly high steps and this helps too.

10. The next encouraging thing that happens is that I start to yawn! This means that the medication has started to work.

11. After that, everything improves. I give several large, loud yawns and my limbs start to function far more normally. I like to shake my arms and legs at this point and I start to walk around more freely.

12. Then, after a few more yawns and stretches I am almost normal again. I feel wonderful at this point and, hey presto, ready to tackle my life anew!

As I have already said, I think that the contributory factors to a difficult 'down' period are: what I have eaten and when; how tired I am and whether I am in a stressful situation.

One thing that I find very helpful in a difficult 'down' is enthusiasm. This can be someone else's enthusiasm or my own. I know that this seems the opposite of the mundane conversation mentioned above, but understanding one's 'downs' becomes an art and different 'downs' require different treatment!

One activity that I really enjoy is teaching French to Jack. We started this at a time when my Parkinson's discomfort was quite strong in the night and it seemed that only this French teaching alleviated it. There have been times, for example at four in the morning, when one would have expected Jack to be a reluctant learner! However, he has persisted heroically and this has definitely helped me in the face of many severe 'downs', particularly when I wasn't used to them. I have found that engaging myself in the role of 'teacher' has given me extra strength to cope with these situations.

Jack feels that his memory has improved since our French sessions started and so I am pleased that the gain has not all been on my side. Also, we have extended the French teaching to various acquaintances and friends, although not at four in the morning!

Another activity that really helps me is if someone is willing to talk to me about abstract subjects. However, I must admit that finding people willing to engage with me in heavy conversation could be difficult. Let us say I suddenly had a significant 'down' in my local supermarket, then one has to be aware of other people's needs and it could cause consternation in some members of the public to be approached by a shaking woman (me) who tries to engage them in a conversation about the nature of consciousness! Standing in a supermarket check-out queue can be enough of a stressful experience for many people without having the added joy of having to respond to those such as myself!

Seriously though, several people with Parkinson's have told me that being engrossed in a subject of great enthusiasm helps them through their worst 'downs' and so I would encourage anyone who has recently been diagnosed with Parkinson's not to give up their interests, projects and passions. One day, these may prove themselves to be of more value than these people had imagined.

17
MOTION

If I were asked to define 'life', my answer would have to include the concept of motion; movement towards one thing and away from another. I cannot think of any aspect of existence that does not include movement. Things, including people, change and this involves moving from one place to another, whether in time, in space or in attitude. By using the word, 'attitude,' I am trying to express the fact that people can change positions psychologically as well as physically.

There are numerous sayings that state the idea that the only thing that we can be sure of is that things will change.

From the Brownian motion of the smallest atomic particles to the unimaginably large orbits of enormous planets and stars, motion is crucial in the description of physical reality. Energy can be converted into mass and mass into energy. This involves motion. Everything involves motion, including human beings.

Human beings need to move, both physically and emotionally. This knowledge is used to persecute people; to hold them, against their will, in institutions such as prisons, possibly in solitary confinement, and generally to make their self-expression as restricted as possible. As the power of the state increases, so, restrictions on the lives of individuals become more possible.

But, we don't need to blame prison wardens or the State for the restraints that Parkinson's Disease places on people. Medical textbooks describe Parkinson's as a disorder of movement and also as a problem with the initiation of movement. I would like to add another description:

'Parkinson's is a state of enforced stillness in a world where movement is necessary for communication and development.'

We are used to the idea that some people want to climb mountains because, 'they are there'. Most children like to skip and hop and jump because they can do so. For the same kinds of reasons people may want to express themselves because they have something to say; because they want to recount something that they have observed, something that is important to them that they wish to impart to others. This is particularly because being understood and having one's ideas and feelings affirmed by others, makes us happy. An example is the spontaneous outpouring of joy that occurs in a Control Centre when a space craft lands where it should, making years of planning worthwhile!

When people first become aware that a friend or a relative has Parkinson's they learn to recognize the trembling, the shaking and the general unsteadiness in the afflicted person, but they are not often aware of the gradual slowing down of the whole of his or her ability to communicate. This change is often embarrassing to you, the Parkinson's sufferer, but is not noticed by most other people. It is when people stop listening to you because your voice sounds somewhat monotonous; when they start finishing your sentences for you because you take too long to say them; and eventually, when they stop hearing what you are trying to express, that you start to feel even more 'different'. It is only a short step from the position of assuming that you don't have a point of view and that of virtually ignoring your existence. People with Parkinson's have told me that at particular points in their Parkinson's lives, they wondered if they had become invisible. Clever assertions and speedy responses are so very much valued as the currency of media communication nowadays that patience and listening are not often noticed as being important.

I have an unclear concept of God and, as yet, no view of 'His' identity. However, recently I heard an idea that I liked. The idea was that originally there was a 'God' and nothing else. However, 'He' needed to communicate and so he created other entities, free in that they were not merely to be his puppets, otherwise his communication with them would have been meaningless. He wanted to experience being the 'Other' as well as the 'Self'. (I am using the word 'self' to mean 'oneself' and 'other' to mean 'another person or people'.)

As soon as a relationship is formed, then the concepts of 'Self' and 'Other' become meaningful and motion becomes an intrinsic part of the relationship. For many people the development of their personalities, of their understanding of themselves, of their experience of reality are outcomes of having the experience of a relationship with another.

Communication between people involves conversation;

exchange of points of view; argument; compromise; enjoyment of the other person's weaknesses as well as their strengths; some understanding of how it feels to be the other person; and attitudes towards each other, together with the changing of such attitudes. There is movement in the emotions; towards and away from the other person or people.

Positive relationships can encompass numerous kinds of friendship; love; sexual interaction. If the encounters between people are of value, both the 'Self' and the 'Other' can develop in directions that they may have previously not recognized as important. For many of us, the nearest we can get to perfect happiness is through a relationship with another. Relationships involve motion.

Of course a relationship can also be antagonistic and stultified. For example, people can be forced to interact when they do not wish to and then relationships can become negative and even dangerous.

Human beings need to express themselves emotionally and artistically, as well as physically. There are many means for self expression and they all involve movement: facial expression, talking, singing, dancing, sign language, writing, painting, music and all the electronic means of communication that are available.

If one contemplates Parkinson's Disease, one becomes aware of stillness, lack of motion, where one would normally have expected movement. This is an enforced stillness that can extend to every aspect of body movement, from ballet dancing to going to the toilet. It seems as if the goal of the malady is to stop movement and communication for the afflicted person, hence separating them from the rest of the population.

The Parkinson's person does not remain still because of a general feeling of peace and tranquility. He or she does not have a blank face because of a lack of emotion or interest. Bodily movement, energetic bustling around, the carrying out enthusiastically of plans, are not absent because of a lack of imagination or creativity. No, the Parkinson's person is in the grip of an iron fist that relentlessly forces that person out of the cycle of movement that whirls the world around.

What that fist is, we still don't know. However, we do know that, with the help of other people, the grip can loosen and the person with Parkinson's can experience at least some initiative, some communication and some joy.

It all depends on other people. As I have tried to describe in this book, other people are immensely important in the world of those who have Parkinson's. Other people can provide the link that restores some motion to the Parkinson's person's life. Medications are invaluable and supplementary therapies can strengthen the Parkinson's person's inner resilience. However, it is the forging of new relationships and the development or transformation of older relationships that can bring back the motion in a Parkinson's person's life. Apparently, Lazarus was raised from the dead. I have the most enormous respect for the people who can raise the Parkinson's person from the experience of enforced stillness to one of joining in the motion of life.

18
SOME PUZZLES

Parkinson's Disease has given me the opportunity to experience some situations that have been new and puzzling to me and have given me food for thought. Here are three examples.

1. Into Bed

About a year ago, when my time since the diagnosis of my PD was around thirteen years, I was finding it increasingly difficult to undress, wash, change into my night-clothes and get into bed at night. The reason was fatigue, to an extent that I had not felt before. This tiredness was definitely not the usual tiredness that I used to feel, at the end of the day, before I had Parkinson's. Neither was it the increased fatigue that I had felt as I progressed through thirteen years of Parkinson's. It was more extreme than that and I gradually realised that it was linked to the mobility of my body. My Parkinson's was now increasingly expressing tiredness in terms of immobility. When I was tired, my movements slowed down and so the more tired I was, the more immobile I became and the harder it was to complete my evening ritual of getting ready to go to bed.

I thought about the situation and came up with an idea…

First of all, I bought myself two pairs of smart pyjamas. Then, I started to wash and change into my chosen night-wear much earlier in the evening than had been my habit. I then re-named the pyjamas, 'evening wear'. So, now I hardly had any washing or changing to do at bed-time because I had spread these tasks over a longer period. It didn't take long for people to accept my new attire if they decided to visit me in the evenings.

However, I still had a problem and that was getting into bed. By the time I was ready for bed I had gathered more fatigue, despite my pyjama routine, so that when I finally tried the apparently simple action of clambering into bed, I could hardly move at all! I would say encouraging phrases to myself such as: 'come on, you're doing well'; ' sit on the bed'; 'well done'; 'try to pull one leg into bed'. But it was no good. My movement would almost stop. Eventually, Jack had to drag me into the bed and this did not fit in with my self-image as a sophisticated person in smart night-attire!

Then, I was talking to a friend at the local Parkinson's Group, who told me that he just points himself at his bed, makes a lunge and somehow manages to get into it, without knowing how. I decided to have a try at this revolutionary (to me) method! I positioned myself appropriately with regard to the bed, said, 'Into bed!' in my mind and lunged. Sure enough, I managed somehow to land in the bed, although not without surprise to Jack! He had been dozing and later said that he had imagined he was being attacked by a lion, when I had landed beside him!

I repeated this procedure, the following night and, this time, I gave Jack a warning first. 'Look out!' worked well!

I carried out the same process every night for about three weeks before trying to analyze what I was doing. When I did analyze my movements, I realized that I was getting into bed using eight movements and always the same eight movements. The secret seemed to be around my saying 'into bed' very fast, until it seemed to be one word only: 'intobed'. My Parkinson's self seemed to understand the instruction as being about one action instead of the eight actions that were really undertaken. Parkinson's could cope with being asked to carry out one action, whereas it couldn't cope with eight actions.

2. The number One

After I had achieved the above method of getting into bed every night, I thought a lot about Parkinson's and the number one. Many people with Parkinson's had told me that, as their condition had developed, they could do fewer and fewer things at any one time. I definitely feel that I can now only do one thing at a time unless I am in a particularly strong 'On' state, when I am sometimes able to do two. The question of what 'one' item means to the brain fascinates me. 'One' is puzzling. For example, in this book, one letter is different from one word and one word is very different from one chapter. Yet, my brain would classify each of them as 'one'. It seems to me that my brain regularly manages to do many things at a time whilst it gives the impression that it is only able to carry out one thing.

The way I explain the above phenomenon to myself is by using a metaphor. I imagine to myself that 'normal' people have a large number of 'communication channels' with the outside world, but that having Parkinson's Disease brings the number of these channels down to one or possibly two. This would explain why people with Parkinson's can do only one thing at a time.

3. *Concrete thinking*

So long as I am 'up' and if I am in a peaceful situation, I can think clearly and can type my thoughts on my laptop. However, I have a problem in trying to organize and communicate my thoughts to others, especially if I am in a noisy, crowded situation. If I try to engage in a discussion in public, I peter out rapidly. But in private, or with someone who understands me well and is patient, I have far less difficulty.

I sometimes tackle the problem of organizing myself and my thoughts by using actual, physical 'concrete' items to do so. In Chapter six of this book, for example, I have given an account of classifying different pieces of paper work and storing them in files or containers so that the information contained within them is easily attainable. I use colour, size and shape to differentiate between containers and hence between jobs. For example, I might have a large red box to represent 'Finances'. (There is always a job to do on Finances!) and a round green tin for 'Ideas'.

As I mentioned in my previous book, when I give a talk, I can't use written notes because I shake so much that I can't read them. So, I use my imagination to represent the talk I want to give. I may imagine a steam train moving across the countryside, with each carriage holding a particular part of the talk. Then, I imagine myself moving from one carriage to another. In that way I can 'read' my talk. As regards thinking, I sometimes 'put' a particular idea on a chair in the room I am in. Then perhaps I'll 'put' another idea on the settee. This is a way of using my visual imagination and visual memory by 'placing' parts of my memory as images outside of my brain and using them to help me to focus on what I am trying to think out.

I find that this 'concrete' way of thinking interlinks with my visual imagination and has helped my memory and my thinking ability. I do not know how or why this has happened, but having Parkinson's Disease has encouraged me to find new, creative ways of doing things and talking about them.

I have found that thinking my way through my Parkinson's 'puzzles' has been a challenging, rewarding and stimulating way of using my brain and I hope that I may develop more of this kind of thinking in the future.

19
WHO AM I?

Descartes said, 'I think, therefore I am'. So, his confidence in his existence, that which gave him his identity, was based on two things: his ability to think and his conviction that it was he who was doing the thinking.

I wonder what Descartes would say today, if he had Parkinson's and was taking levodopa? Would he say, 'We think, therefore I am?'

As a person with Parkinson's, who takes strong, brain-altering drugs, I wonder at times what is me and what is the effect of the drugs I take, particularly because each drug has a long list of possible side-effects.

The Parkinson's that I experience at present (in my fourteenth year since diagnosis), is a condition of extreme opposites. I live in several physical states that are very different from each other. For example, I frequently experience the highly irritating sensation of shaking uncontrollably. When I am in this state I become very clumsy and I would advise anyone who has delicate, valuable possessions to keep them well out of my reach! I cannot write when I am like this. I am pretty sure that this state is simply me (plus Parkinson's) and is not caused by my drugs.

On the other hand, I can suddenly and mysteriously change into a kind of statue that can hardly move. Parkinson's particular way of expressing fatigue is through the loss of mobility. My level of fatigue is increased by stress, physical exertion and even talking a lot (in my case a very likely occurrence!). Even thinking, in the sense of logically thinking out a problem, also contributes to my fatigue. When all of these pressures bear down together on me, I can be made motionless. However, when I emerge from this state; when I come back to life, as it were, I feel that this is partly a result of my taking some rest and partly a result of two of the medications I take; levodopa and Pramipexole.

My first experience of immobility, owing to exhaustion, did not occur until I had had Parkinson's for thirteen years. On that occasion, Jack and I were in France and had returned home late, having spent a busy few hours with a new acquaintance. I felt very tired, lay down on the bed and ... could not move. The only thing I could do was speak! I interpreted what was happening to me as being some kind of psychological trauma. I did not interpret my symptoms as deriving from Parkinson's. Eventually, I asked Jack if he would ring John and Mary, two very long-standing friends of ours, in England. I thought that if they would engage with me in talking about some of the situations we had experienced together, particularly if they had been amusing situations, then the familiarity might bring me back to normal; I was still interpreting what was happening to me as having a psychological cause. (Never self-diagnose!). So, Jack rang the UK and got through to John. We talked on the phone and, after about a quarter of an hour, I started being able to move again and was back to 'normal' within a further quarter of an hour. I now realize that my state of immobility was due to exhaustion and since then I have had several similar experiences, only they were less dramatic and did not last as long as in the first situation.

My third physical state is one of dyskinesia; involuntary movements. In this state I may rock from side to side in what appears an exaggerated manner and at times I become over-active. I also feel very fun-loving and optimistic when I am in this dyskinesic state. I feel that my persona; the personality I am showing at that time, is mainly an effect of one of the drugs that I take. However, I am not sure if this is the only explanation because I have only recently developed dyskinesias and so I am only just starting to observe this state in myself. I assume that dyskinesias occur when the amount of levodopa available at a particular time is too much for the body to cope with. I have found that relaxation can be helpful in calming down my dyskinesias.

My fourth state is one of 'normality'(which I interpret as being me and Parkinson's). However, as described in Chapter One of this book, my 'normal' state is not as normal as before I contracted Parkinson's. I have a continual feeling of being out of balance, rather like a mild giddiness, and I try not to take any risks when walking, for fear of falling. I can write when I am in this physical state although not as tidily as in the past.

I almost forgot to describe my fifth state which is one of

being in pain. I now experience pain more frequently when I go 'Off' or 'down'. I find that relaxation helps.

Taking all the above states of being in mind at once, no wonder people find it difficult to understand PD. I find it difficult to understand! (I'm sure that even Descartes would be confused!) I can feel awful at one part of the day and then bounce enthusiastically into a gathering at another part of the day, where I am continually told how well I look!

At times I can walk upright and at other times I am bent over; a very old woman indeed. I can speak with a loud voice and then, later on, I can only manage a whisper. The behaviour of those with Parkinson's must puzzle others. For example, I expect that some people must think, 'She could do it yesterday and so, with a little effort, surely she could do it today'. Well, no, difficult as it may be to understand, 'she' cannot !

As a Parkinson's person, I do not live out my days smoothly, following a continuous line but rather in jerky, abruptly changing steps. Currently I can be in an 'On' phase with all the capabilities that go with it, and then, after a few small tremors, my right arm can start to shake vigorously and I deteriorate quickly to being 'Off'. This radical change now occurs within about four minutes. Another difficulty for others to understand is that some of my requirements are immediate. I cannot wait around for my medication when it is due, for example. I need it now.

Descartes pronounced confidently, 'I am'. But, I have to go a little further and ask, 'Who am I?' I have often wondered whether what I learned about myself over the years, before I developed PD, is now redundant. Are the answers to who am I, now completely different?

When I was very young, during my first eight years or so, I hardly knew myself at all. I reacted to events. But, with the influence of reading (I read avidly from a young age), getting to know other people, life changes and occasionally realizing to my surprise that some people had positive expectations of me that I would never have imagined of myself, I gradually constructed a view of my personality. Learning was very important to me; at first studying a mish-mash of subjects and then Science, and finally Psychology with its accompanying therapy and supervision. (People who work in professions that involve counseling others need to know themselves very well and in my case I had regular psychological therapy for several years for this reason.) With all these experiences, my view of myself became fuller and hopefully more accurate. However, never in my wildest dreams did I imagine that one day I would become a disabled person who would at times look odd and shake violently whilst at other times I would not be able to move and would very much depend on others for everyday living.

Is it possible to continue to develop as a human being, including learning more about oneself, about other people and about the world in general, despite having a severe disability ?

I can honestly say, yes, I have found it so.

For example, one way that I have developed during my

fourteen years with Parkinson's is that I have gained significantly in self confidence. It does indeed take self-confidence to have dyskinesias in public, to walk in an ungainly manner and, horror of horrors, to dribble!

Hemingway is reputed to have said that the difference between the poor and the rich is that the rich have more money. Similarly, the difference between the disabled and the able-bodied is that the able-bodied have more ability (physical and/or mental) to reach for and gain what they want. Otherwise, the needs of both groups are surely similar: to spend their lives in a manner that fulfills them; to consider others, (if they have the insight to realize how fulfilling this will be for them); to be happy.

There is no easy answer to the question, Who am I? but there can be great joy in trying to find out. 'Finding out' does not mean 'Putting up with the status quo'. It means taking action, making decisions, causing change. Yes, and even if one has Parkinson's!

20
COMMUNICATION

I have come to the end of the second book on the development of my Parkinson's Disease and I feel a little sad. First of all, I will miss writing about my experiences. Of course I hardly ever write (my Parkinson's stops me doing that), instead I type on my laptop. However, both writing and typing give me the opportunity to put my ideas into words and as E.M.Forster is credited to have said, 'How can I tell what I mean till I see what I say?' Perhaps some of those who read my books will be encouraged to put their own experience of Parkinson's into words.

My other reason for sadness, at the end of writing this book, is that I will miss feeling a kind of link with so many people who are taking on the challenges of Parkinson's, particularly if they are on their own or feel alone. As I have already emphasized, I feel that Parkinson's is a condition where other people can significantly improve one's lot or make it much worse.

I can offer no medical suggestions as to how we go forwards with finding a cure, or more effective medication for Parkinson's, because I am not a doctor, nor a researcher. However, I am a person with Parkinson's and I can offer my account of how PD makes me feel, physically and emotionally, how I do my best to live with these feelings and what improves matters for me when I am 'Off' or 'down.'

From my first trembles, through the various surprises which Parkinson's has brought me over the years, I have tried to convey my personal feelings of having the condition, the reality of it, and I intend and hope to continue to do so in the future.

I feel a bit like an explorer. Parkinson's is such an unusual illness and I hope that by leaving markers, as I progress through the condition, these will help others to make sense of what they are experiencing if or when they get there.

When we are first diagnosed as having Parkinson's, it is by a medical person. So, naturally, it is to the medical people that we turn for advice. Very quickly we learn that our illness is not yet curable, although it can substantially be helped, using Western methods. On the whole, this means taking medication: orally; by injection; via a patch; or through a pump that is fixed to the body, slowly releasing the medication directly into the blood stream. Although this treatment is extremely successful for most people with Parkinson's in the first few years, it gradually becomes less efficient, over time, at doing its job of trying to make up for the lack of dopamine in the brain.

This puts us and the 'medics' in an unusual position. There is no easy answer as regards treatment, after the first few years. It is a matter of trial and error and it would seem likely that the best results come when doctor and patient work together. This can be very difficult if the doctor, the patient or both have problems in communicating with each other.

Communication with Parkinson's people can be difficult

because of a diminished ability to express ourselves verbally and also because some of us talk in whispers, to the point of being inaudible. These are common traits and such Parkinson's people need to be given time to find the words they need. Anyone communicating with them needs to have patience and to be a good listener. Optimism is a must. The sentence, 'nothing can be done for you' (as quoted to me by some Parkinson's patients, from their experience) should be banned! For one reason, it is not true and for another, it is cruel. There are many helpful supplementary modes of medicine as well as those administered via classical methods.

I have been fortunate with the medical people who have worked with me. They have done just that; worked **with** me. For example, I was highly impressed a couple of months ago when my GP asked me how it felt to be taking the drug, Pramipexole. He sat back in his chair and listened while I tried to describe the effects that the drug has on me. In the same way as I get to know people and the effect they have on me, I have found that I get to know my drugs and their effects on me as well. I have used 'The Chart' (see Chapter 11) to do so. This information can sometimes be used as a source of feedback for medical staff.

My message to everyone with Parkinson's is that if one can resist the natural instinct to hide away from people because of embarrassment, there is a whole world out there waiting for Parkinson's people's involvement. I am not trying to trivialize embarrassment, just come and watch me looking odd and you will understand that!

People with Parkinson's have much to offer others with the condition. After all, many of them have lived with Parkinson's for a number of years and so they have information that could help others who have not had PD for as long. I feel that Parkinson's people should be consulted more by 'medics' about the methods used to cope with the changeability, the discomfort and the pain of Parkinson's. I also feel that it would be very valuable if we Parkinson's persons expressed ourselves to each other and exchanged ideas more often.

I would be really pleased if the treatment for Parkinson's included providing training rather than just taking medication. Artistic skills are already used to help people with Parkinson's, for example, singing, painting, drawing and dancing. I should like a system to be developed where we were also taught, (or more accurately, re-taught), communication skills to regain the technique of taking part in two-way conversations. I, personally, would also value regular training in computing, the use of the mobile 'phone, and other information technology. Even a basic knowledge of these areas could open up the life of someone with Parkinson's. One of the reasons that I am suggesting the importance of training is because I feel that the intellectual abilities of people with Parkinson's can easily be under-estimated. I feel that the lack of communication skills in the Parkinson's person is the main factor causing this underestimation of their abilities. Just because someone is quiet, even very quiet, this does not mean that they cannot think. They may need other people in order to explain their thinking, but this is a simple matter compared with coming up with the thoughts in the first place.

I have been helped a lot in adjusting to all the recent changes in myself by two of the Parkinson's support groups, which meet in our area of London. Parkinson's groups differ in size, but the group with which I have been the longest is large, around eighty people with Parkinson's, who meet for various activities, together with their partners or carers. Quite apart from the fact that these people are very pleasant to know, there is the fact that they have Parkinson's and look as though they have Parkinson's. It is an excellent feeling, being among one's own. It makes me feel relaxed and accepted. What I particularly like about this group is that by meeting regularly, we slowly get to know each other, in a natural way, genuinely building up relationships. Also, people in the groups I have mentioned above are particularly supportive to anyone who is going through a bad patch.

The title of this book describes both Parkinson's and myself as having made progress along our different paths. That is true. To try to measure who or which has made the most progress, is difficult, but I think it is me (I may be biased!). For, although Parkinson's continually attempts to push forward, I assert my rights in as many ways as I can find, to live as normally as possible.

Let me leave you, temporarily I hope, with a thought and then with an image.

Here is the thought:

'Conversation is far more than an exchange of words.'

Here is the image:

I like to imagine being on a slide, to imagine myself, sitting calm and relaxed on a mat, which is careering down an endless chute. Things may be changing around me, frighteningly fast, but so long as I can maintain my position on that mat, there will be no damage to myself.

Well, I can always hope!